# Horsemanship 101

## BUILDING THE FOUNDATION

### AUGUSTUS M WALTON

❀ Created with Vellum

In your Horsemanship Planner, you'll have...

- Tool List
- Horse Assessment
- Lesson Planner/Progress Tracker
- Vet Checks
- Farrier Schedule
- Nutrition Tracker

# BOOK 1

Building A Foundational Relationship

# Introduction

Horsemanship is an age-old skill passed down from generation to generation, and the term refers to any equestrian sport, as well as caring for, training, and riding horses. Understanding these magnificent creatures and how they think is essential when it comes to quality horsemanship.

When you send your child to kindergarten for the first time, you automatically assume their teacher is knowledgeable in all things kindergarten, right? How else will she do her job? Arming yourself with proper horsemanship technique and knowledge of your horse's psychology will be your biggest superpower when it comes to building a relationship with your horse. Knowledge leads to confidence, confidence leads to respect, respect leads to control, and finally, control means you get to have fun with your horse safely.

In earlier years, horses were mainly used for labor, in which training methods were more focused on fast results rather than lasting results. Rushed training makes for a sloppy, fearful, dangerous horse. It's so important to remember horses are living, breathing creatures, which means they have their own minds, thoughts, and reactions. If you don't understand what makes your horse do the things he does, you will always struggle in your horsemanship journey. Horses can either make you feel like you are on top of the world or hopeless in a bottomless pit. I promise it's much easier to pick yourself up, brush off the dust and continue through the challenges when you know why things are happening a certain way.

This book series offers you the light at the end of the tunnel, educating you on your horse's basic needs and psychology, and arming you with knowledge and methods to identify the problem and move forward with solving it. Remember this famous saying: *"Frustration begins where knowledge ends."* Fill up your knowledge box so you can solve any problem you have with any horse.

# *Principles of Horsemanship*

At its roots, horsemanship principles are based on prey vs. predator behavior. Simply put, horsemanship is a respectful relationship and common language between you and your horse.

The principles we are focusing on include:

- Respect – having respect for your horse and gaining your horse's respect. Don't act like a predator, and your horse won't act like prey.
- Make no assumptions – assume your horse knows nothing.
- Communication is vital – establish a common, consistent language. Body language is universal; pay attention.
- First, horses teach humans, then humans teach horses – start at the appropriate level according to your knowledge and experience.
- Feel and timing – this comes with time and experience.

1

- Humans and horses have mutual responsibilities – respecting each other.
- Pressure – make them so uncomfortable they have to move their feet.
- Positive reinforcement – reward your horse with the release of pressure when they move in even the slightest.

## RIDER AND HORSE RELATIONSHIP

The main goal here is for the rider and the horse to become attuned to each other's physical and mental needs in order to experience mutual benefits. A basic understanding of your horse's behavior makes for a better learning experience. Horses are highly reactive and instinctual. Knowing how your horse thinks and processes information helps maintain everyone's safety, and being able to differentiate between normal and abnormal behavior gives a deeper understanding of the relationship.

I don't have the words to express to you how much my relationship with my horses means to me, nor could I count the numerous life lessons they have taught me. The process of building this relationship is definitely challenging, but for you as a beginner, the rewards are far beyond what you can imagine.

## HORSE BEHAVIOR

. . .

Naturally, horses are prey animals. Fight-or-flight mode is a built-in survival trait. Horses' remarkable perceptiveness can be commonly misunderstood as "spooky" or bad behavior. In addition, horses have a very quick response time to react to a perceived danger. While all of this is natural behavior, horses can be desensitized from these reactions. Gaining your horse's trust will ensure you are able to assist him in quickly learning what is dangerous and harmless. We want all training experiences to be positive, so we need to apply knowledge to the situation.

Categorizing experiences into fight-or-flight reactions, horses may need to be shown many times that something is harmless. We need to understand horses win leadership roles within their herds by controlling the movement of their fellow horses. Moreover, horses accept a loss of leadership when; applied pressure causes them to move or when applied pressure inhibits movement. Attention to body language is essential to becoming an effective horse trainer.

If a horse's tail is held
  High – you know they are alert.
  Low – you know they are submitting to you; they are exhausted, afraid, or in pain.
  Extra high – usually, a foal will display this way; this tells us they are playful, or danger mode is on high alert.
  We can assume a bit of irritation (most likely caused by flies).

If a horse's legs are
  Pawing – we know they are frustrated or being impatient.

Stomping – they are indicating a mild threat.

Back leg lifted – can be a defensive threat to kick.

If a horse's ears are

Neutral – they are held loosely up, facing forward or out. We know the horse is relaxed.

Pricked – stiff ears, held directly out, says the horse is alert.

Airplane ears – facing outward, drooping down, show the horse is tired or in pain.

Ears angled back – (towards rider) show they are attentive to the rider and commands.

Ears pinned flat – this horse is angry and could react aggressively. Watch out!

Something important to remember here is that a horse's behavior depends on multiple things, such as proper nutrition, efficient space (stall, barn, etc.), enough exercise, breed, and temperament. Like you and me, you can't expect a good attitude if even one of these lacks your proper attention.

## BAD HABITAT FORMS BAD HABIT

These habits can occur when the horse is improperly kept – meaning the horse is malnourished, the stall is too small, the horse is lonely, has inadequate exercise, or is subjected to abusive behavior by the owner.

Being able to spot these "bad" behaviors in a horse gives you an advantage in the training process.

. . .

Cribbing – this is when a horse bites a surface, like a stall, doors edge, or fence, pulling and curving his neck, sucking in air. Endorphins are released in the brain, giving the horse temporary relief from the unpleasant situation. Cribbing can lead to weight loss, poor performance, colic, and tooth loss.

Weaving – this is a horse rhythmically shifting its weight on the front legs while swinging the head back and forth. It is usually caused by boredom or excess energy (insufficient exercise), causing weight loss and weak tendons.

Wood chewing – this can be seen as eating bedding, dirt, or self-mutilation, caused by boredom, lack of exercise, or malnutrition. You can provide free-choice salts or minerals and freedom to graze to help decrease this urge.

A basic understanding of horse biology and nutrition is another essential tool for your knowledge box. Let me break it down for you. Horses have six basic nutrient needs:

- Carbohydrates are broken into two categories – structural (fiber) and non-structural (sugar/starch). The roughage in the diet, such as hay, grass, etc., is full of both. The quality of your hay is essential; too coarse or too fine can cause digestive issues. Horses' digestive tracts have evolved to support a roughage-based diet, so extras like grain, oats, etc., should only be used for supplementing or meeting nutritional requirements.

- Protein – is necessary for maintenance and growth. Let's bust a myth here: "The higher the protein, the higher the energy of the horse." Ehhhhh, wrong! Proteins are actually most difficult to break down and convert to usable energy. Protein is beneficial during rapid growth, lactating mares, gestation period in pregnant mares, or during intense training or competing. Horses need between 12–18% protein. You get these proteins from sac feed. The percentages are always listed. Read them. Decide what percent your horse requires, based on needs and the job at hand.

- Fat – this is an easily-digested source of energy. Horses can handle a relatively high amount of fat in their diet, making it more available to convert to energy. How is fat added to their feed? Stabilized oils – you can buy feed supplemented with fat. These feeds usually contain 2–4% fat, or you can add your own supplements to your regular feed and control the percentage. It's essential to note adding fat will decrease the amount of feed required. This means you have to be sure the rest of the nutritional needs are being met as well.

- Vitamins – these are critical; they absolutely must be present. There are two types of vitamins:
- Water-soluble vitamins, B complex. You need to know you can't really overdo water-soluble

vitamins because they are excreted through the urine.

- Fat-soluble vitamins A, E, D, and K definitely can be overdone because they are stored in the animals' fat tissue, meaning excessive amounts will build up toxicity. A good forage program, combined with a commercial feed, usually covers all the bases.

- Minerals – are critical to the horses' function. These needs change, depending on your horses' stage and situation in life. Again this is something achievable with good forage and commercial feed.

- Water – obviously a necessity. Quality water is a massive factor in hydration and digestion. Don't even waste your money on supplements and vitamins if you can't offer nice, clean, quality water to your horse.

## PRINCIPLES OF BEHAVIORAL TRAINING

Primarily, behavioral principles are based on inherited traits and environmental influences. Two people are the primary influence of these principles: the breeder governing heredity such as bloodlines and temperament, and the trainer in control of the environment, who is responsible for performance. The horse's performance in some ways depends on the breed of the horse. For example, a hot-blooded horse, who is usually high energy in nature, will require less pressure to move his feet than a cold-blooded horse, who is usually a little lazy and requires more pressure to move his feet. Knowing your horses' breed and temperament will help the training process to be less frustrating due to misunderstanding your horses' actions and reactions. We are modifying our horses' actions, not changing their inherited nature.

What behavioral problems arise in hot-blooded horses, such as thoroughbreds, Arabians, and some quarter horses? These guys are very athletic, intelligent, quick learners, and a lot more sensitive to their environment. This makes them very reactive and more likely to be spooky, jumpy, and faster in nature. Let's say you take your hot-blooded horse on a trail ride. Your attention to your horse's body language will always cue you in on the actions and reactions. I tell you this because, on this horse, you better be watching. Little things like a bag blowing in the wind, a shiny object, an oncoming car, or even just a fellow trail rider coming up behind you – these are all potential hazards. When it comes to pace, you definitely won't be at the back of the pack. This can be a problem if you don't have control of his feet. He may be prancing, whinnying, bobbing his head up and down, ignoring your commands to slow down. These behavioral problems are all solvable. Don't let that sway you away from hot-blooded horses, instead use that information to make an educated decision on what type of horse better suits you and your needs.

Moving on to cold-blooded horses and their potential behavioral problems – these horses are usually more level-headed, kind, relaxed, gentle in nature, docile, slower learners.

Let's ride out on the same trail with our cold-blooded horse. You should always pay attention to your horse's body language, but in this case, you are likely to be more relaxed and move much slower. This can be good, but the problems are usually having to put more energy into getting him to move and keeping up the pace. Your horse may need to be kicked or smooched repeatedly to keep pace, may sling his head when asked to move out; he will try any which way to avoid doing work before giving in to your command. Both of these situations could be extremely frustrating to the person with zero knowledge of the horses' breed and nature. Punishment is hardly ever an effective way of correcting behavior, mostly because lack of consistent common language is the primary culprit. Simply put, your horse likely has no idea what you want from him, and you have no idea how to tell him, so beating him only creates more significant problems. Respect is a massive player in behavior. We'll talk more about this later.

How do I go about dealing with behavioral issues?

- Understand the breed.
- Educate yourself on horse psychology.
- Apply pressure-and-release method.

Of course, it is not this simple when we put it into action, but I can guarantee taking the time to learn these 3 points will save you and your horse hours upon hours of frustration.

## SAFETY

. . .

Horses are big animals, weighing anything from 900 to 2,000 pounds. You can be seriously injured or even killed if you don't know how to be safe around your horse. Understanding how your horse thinks is imperative to safety. You should be more hyper-aware of the surroundings and learn what could cause your horse to spook. You will be able to take preventative measures that could save you both from injury. You should always wear proper attire when dealing with horses. Jeans and boots protect your skin from rubbing and getting chapped and your feet from getting stomped. A correctly-tied halter ensures your horse won't get loose, while the lead should be tied to break away in case the horse sets back. We don't want our horse ever to set back and break a lead if we can avoid it. This leads to bigger, more dangerous problems. Having proper knowledge when it comes to tacking up your horse keeps you safe on and off the ground. You want to establish a personal bubble, and your horse is not allowed in unless invited. You can do this by moving his feet away from you when he gets too close and releasing pressure when he's out of your space.

Never approach the horse from his blind spots:

- Directly behind him – if you spook the horse by approaching him in his blind spot, his reaction may be to kick you or run over the top of you because he can't see you.
- Directly in front of him – because horses' eyes are on the sides of their faces, they cannot see directly in front of them without turning a bit to either

side. Spooking him from here could result in him slinging his head and knocking you down, running forward right over you, or if he's tied, he could set back and ultimately hurt himself.

I'm going to share three levels of comfort for your horse with you. You should know when and where these zones are for your horse to ensure everyone's safety.

- Comfortable – A general rule is that your horse's comfort zone is where he is relaxed and happy, most likely in a familiar place, around the barn or paddock, or near other horses. He's able to operate his thinking brain in these spaces. This space feels safe and comfortable, allowing him to be more relaxed in order for him to pay attention to you and what you are teaching. He is also more available to soak up the lesson because he's not concerned with his surroundings. These areas are perfect for learning new things. Generally, this is where you should spend most of your time.

- A bit uncomfortable – This space is slightly unfamiliar; this can cause the horse to feel anxious or nervous. He will be more aware of sounds and objects. This leaves less available attention to you. You need to become more aware of your surroundings and potential hazards, as well as pay extra attention to your horse's body language –

how's his breathing? What are his ears doing? At this point, we want to get his feet moving to keep his thinking brain more prominent than the reactive brain. These areas are not so sure spaces and should be visited for a short time only.

- Danger – At this point, your horse assumes his life is in danger, and he is in fight-or-flight mode, operating in the reactive brain. He is no longer paying any attention to you or your commands. Ideally, we want to avoid any of these dangerous places. These areas are unfamiliar or even tight spaces that put him into fight-or-flight mode and should be avoided for safety at this time.

It would be beneficial for you to go ahead and identify all of these places. Anywhere you go with your horse, pay particular attention to his different zones of comfort. I found it helpful actually to write this down, and it enabled me to create a map of all the areas we worked in together. From my map, I was able to work out my horse's trouble areas. This gave me a more in-depth look at my horse and the issues I needed to work out. Remember, everything with your horse can be worked out with time and consistent application of Pressure and Release method. Slowly working up to big scary things is only beneficial to you both if it's done with patience and care to ensure the safety of all.

. . .

As you move in and out of the comfortable space to the slightly uncomfortable space from time to time, you will notice your horse expanding his comfort zone. This should be done at a slow and safe pace, but eventually, the slightly uncomfortable space will be a completely comfortable space, and you will find yourself on the edge of what used to be the danger zone. This accomplishment is worth celebrating!

*Psychology*

## COMMON LANGUAGE

The first thing we have to talk about is communication. This is a common issue among horse owners. The problem is not having clear, consistent language for communicating to each other what one wants. More often than not, this inability to connect leads to criticism, frustration, or the horse being punished. Beating the horse for not knowing what to do only causes more confusion and resentment in the horse. This is not healthy for building relationships.

I want you to think of your horse as a small child – full of energy, intelligent, capable, and requiring clear, simple, under-standable direction. Start with simple tasks, gradually adding harder, more extended exercises. This will also help establish your common language, cementing it with clear, consistent direction. If you ask your toddler to read you a book without first teaching them the alphabet, then sounds, and so on, there is a 99.9% chance they won't be able to read the book. You have to teach your horse what you want them to know with broken-down, digestible lessons. Hand signals, body language, and the Pressure and Release method are your language-building tools.

Training a horse is about paying attention to the feel of your horse, your timing of releasing pressure from your horse, and the experience of these two together. This is also the foundation of your common language. Time and consistency is your best friend when training a horse. Your child isn't born able to tell you what's wrong or what's bothering them, yet we are always able to satisfy their needs. View horses the same way. You don't have another option but to pay attention and use the process of elimination to find what works.

PREY VS PREDATOR

Moreover, horses operate in the prey mindset. This is important to know when it comes to training your horse because this is how we analyze their actions, reactions, and behavior. Horses have 360° vision. This is so they can quickly spot a predator. They have only two blind spots, one being right in front of the nose, the other, right behind the tail. When something comes up behind your horse, and he spooks out of nowhere, it's because he's been genuinely surprised due to the blind spot. Additionally, horses have what's called monocular vision, which means they can't focus in and out on one thing or another as we can. This leaves them with poor depth perception. Have you ever noticed your horse start to bob his head up and down before he crosses a creek or a fallen tree? He's using the refracting sunlight in his eye to measure how high or low his step needs to be. Knowing this gives you the perspective of your horse in this situation. Instead of reprimanding the horse for not crossing right away or mistaking the head bob for disobedience, you are patiently waiting for your horse to adjust, resulting in the desired outcome.

Back to horses being prey animals – this fact means horses' brains are split into two sides. I'll tell you right now that you might as well treat them like two different horses, because there is no guarantee what you taught on one side will carry over to the other side. The rule of thumb is: anything you do on the left side, you must also do on the right side. When horses react in fear, they have two modes, fight or flight. First, the horse decides if what has caught his attention is dangerous to him. If it is, the response is flight. Move, getaway, RUN! If the horse isn't able to escape the said situation, fight mode kicks in. Kick, bite, rear up, back up, break the lead – whatever it takes to fight off the danger. Unfortunately, this imminent danger we speak of could be as harmless as a bag drifting on the breeze. In this situation, proactive awareness is critical. You have to be able to feel the vibe, notice all the variables around you both. Is it windy? Could something get knocked off the trailer and spook the horse? Is there anything the horse could injure themselves on if fight-or-flight mode kicks in?

These are all questions you need to ask yourself, wherever you and your four-legged friend are.

When it comes to people, we tend to force ourselves and our desires onto situations. This is true in our horsemanship journey as well. Learning to not act like a predator helps your horse to not act like a prey animal. Approaching your horse requires patience and respect. Waiting for your horse to show you he's comfortable with the situation before you continue to move toward him is teaching your horse he can trust you.

## PECKING ORDER

Horses are herd animals, and herds organize themselves in a pecking order. It's the ladder of authority. You're probably thinking: *Why is this important? I don't own a herd of horses!* Understanding this gives you perspective into your horse's thought process. You can better understand why your horse does the things he does. Remember the kindergarten teacher? If she doesn't know how 3-4-year-olds learn and process information, what basis does she have on which to teach?

When we observe a herd of horses out in the pasture, we can easily spot Number One. This horse moseys on over to every other horse in the pasture, seemingly pestering them until they move. What's really happening here is, Number One is making it known that he is the leader. He does this by making them move their feet, and he controls them. The game goes like this: *You move, you lose.* For survival instincts, he makes his leadership known. And in the case of imminent danger, everyone knows to follow his direction.

The order can change from day to day. Number One usually is pretty constant, while Two and Three and so on are constantly fighting for higher rank, making it more likely to change often. There are many ways to accomplish this – biting, kicking, or rearing up is most common. The further down the rank the horse is, the less enjoyable his life, you could say. The last horse is the last to drink, the last to eat, last in the walking line, and the first to be preyed upon out in the wild.

When you begin working with your horse, you will inevitably experience him testing you. Would you think your horse was misbehaving or being disrespectful if he came up and nibbled on you? Of course you would – if you had no knowledge of the horse's nature. They will naturally test limits and boundaries. You can think of this as their process of elimination to figure out what you want from them, rather than assuming they are misbehaving. If you can imagine you are saddling your horse, you throw your pad on and turn around to grab your saddle only to find the pad on the ground. You set the saddle down, grab the pad, and reset it. You turn around to grab the saddle and happen to see your sneaky horse reach around and pull it just enough to slide down to the ground. I hope you chuckle, because when I saw this actually happen, I couldn't stop laughing. Mainly because this horse was about 19 years old and was notorious for these kinds of stunts, he was a therapy horse at a dude ranch. He knew these people had little to no experience, and because he understood this, he was able to use his pecking order instincts, testing every rider to see what he could get away with. He knew right away when an experienced rider was on him, leaving him less comical.

Because you now understand your horse's actions are part of his nature, you can remove emotion to avoid taking it personally, eliminating anger and frustration from the situation. In this sense, your horse is not misbehaving, but rather, just behaving naturally.

. . .

## MOTIVATION

What motivates us as humans? Things like being recognized for our hard work, our peers praising us for our accomplishments, as well as acquiring material things. These things motivate us to keep working through challenges, bumps in the road, and self-doubt.

Your horse is intelligent and needs to be mentally and physically stimulated during your lessons. A horse will become bored and unmotivated if the training is too consistent or predictable. They will pick up on this and try to find a way to avoid the work. It can also go the other way. If the training is too random or scattered, they will be confused as to what exactly you expect of them. These two need to be well balanced in order to keep a motivated, attentive, teachable 'student'.

Something else to consider is this: horses love to move their feet. Making sure your horse has enough room to move about and gets enough exercise is crucial for a good attitude. Imagine sitting in a chair at work all day, your body is stiff, your circulation is just getting moving, then your boss tells you to run a 2-mile race right now, or you're fired... You probably won't be jumping with excitement and joy at the thought of this task, much less actually doing it. Not to mention the possibility of hurting yourself due to improper preparation of the mind and body.

. . .

The same goes for your horse. The proper physical and mental state of the horse is a priority. In addition, rewarding your horse for doing what you ask is probably the biggest motivator for your four-legged friend. We do this using the Pressure and Release method. I want to encourage you to set small goals which you know you can accomplish. This will set you up for a confidence boost and give you the motivation to reach the next small goal. I found that in life if we look at a problem and attempt to solve it as a whole, the amount of time and energy it will take can be disheartening and feel impossible. Training a horse is one of these big, long problems we need to solve. Instead of setting yourself up for failure trying to climb the entire mountain, break it up into small achievable hills.

That brings us to our attitude. You will move mountains in your horsemanship journey if you can remember this and apply it. And it goes like this: *If you want to change your horse's reactions, you must first change your own actions.* You may need to work on yourself some before you get into the training.

I know when I started offering my training services at the public pens where I used to keep my horses, I was not prepared at all. I could ride a horse really well, but I had no idea how to do the groundwork. And groundwork, if you didn't know, is the foundation of horse training. I had set myself up to fail, and I did. My first client paid me upfront for one month. Instead of using the money to educate myself on horse psychology or horse training, I decided to wing it. This did not work out for me. By the end of the month, I had lost all confidence in myself, and the horse was no better than when we started. The client was not very happy, but because he had seen me ride horses, no one else could, He allowed me a second chance and paid for a second month. This time I invested my money in a video training course on groundwork. After this, I kicked myself in the butt for not educating myself sooner. In the end, I had many horses to practice with, and eventually, people were lining up for me to do the groundwork on their horses.

The fact that you are here looking for answers says you already have one foot through the door of change!

## TWO HORSES IN ONE

Think of your horse's brain as 'Lefty' and 'Righty.' They are two different horses; messages of experience do not cross over. Just because you have taught something to Lefty does not guarantee Righty caught the drift. Moreso, a 5-minute desensitizing exercise with Lefty could be a 30-minute desensitizing exercise with Righty. Recognizing this could help avoid frustration, confusion, or being mistaken for bad behavior. It only makes sense to teach them independently.

I used to own a barrel horse that had to be saddled from the right side only; this is not the correct side to saddle from, but if I tried to throw it on from the left side, he would blow up straight into fight-or-flight mode, and if we were at a rodeo you could forget running, because everything spooked him the rest of the day. This horse operated in the thinking brain 95% of the time. Whatever trauma he experienced to create this reaction caused him to stay in the reactive brain until the next day. The supposed trauma could be a range of experiences, from just one time spooking at the saddle and being allowed to continue that behavior by being rewarded by saddling from the right side only... to spooking from the saddle and being severely punished for it.

He was a fantastic horse, apart from that one problem. Unfortunately, at that time in my horsemanship journey, I had no knowledge of Lefty and Righty, so instead of solving the problem, I accepted his behavior, allowing him to think that was okay.

This makes your horse think he has a chance at the Number One spot in the pecking order (your spot), which will lead to more disobedience in an attempt to be Number One. This was true as well with old Homer. When I first stepped on him, he would test me by moving in every direction but the one I commanded. After some kicking and smooching, he lost the battle of the feet. Remember – *Whoever moves first loses*. It is crucial for you to be black and white about this: *"I am Number One. You are Number Two."*

Additionally, the mind is categorized into a 'thinking brain' and a 'reactive brain.' The thinking brain presents as calm, relaxed, and attentive to you. Imagine this brain as a muscle. The more you work it, the bigger it gets. We want this brain to overshadow the reactive brain. The reactive brain presents as flighty, spooky, jumpy, sensitive, very reactive. The breed plays a role here, going back to hot-blooded and cold-blooded. Some horses are naturally more reactive; that's okay. Working that muscle will grow the thinking brain and become the driving force.

. . .

How can I grow the thinking brain?

- Controlling his feet – making the horse move when you command.
- Desensitizing – removing the fear of objects in his environment.
- Applying Pressure and Release method.

An exercise called "Draw" consists of you giving the horse your two eyes, capturing the attention of his two eyes, and then withdrawing your look while walking backward, encouraging the horse to follow, making the horse think, using his natural curiosity to get those feet moving toward you.

The reactive brain is more beneficial for the horse's survival instincts, and you cannot breed or work this entirely out. No matter how broke your horse is, it is always possible for them to use the reactive side in any given situation. Thankfully, attention to body language will always give us a heads up.

PSYCHOLOGICAL BENEFITS OF THE RIDER

Studies have shown horses have a positive effect on a list of mental disorders such as:

- Depression

- Anxiety
- Trauma
- Dissociative disorders.

Horses have also been known to lower stress levels and regulate emotions by mirroring yours, showing you what you are putting out there. Buck Brannaman, the leading American horse trainer, once said, *"The horse is a mirror to your soul; sometimes you like what you see, sometimes you don't."* I couldn't agree with this more.

Building a trusting relationship with a horse offers people who have experienced trauma at the hands of a human a chance to receive well-deserved healing. Riding horses has been shown to build up confidence, self-esteem, assertiveness, and emotional regulation. In my own experience, horses have always been my therapy. As a child, I was repeatedly sexually abused by a family member. While the culprit lived right next door to me, making it impossible to escape, my horses were readily available in the barn behind our houses, offering me a temporary way out. Having a trusting confidant, even in an animal, was life-saving. When I got on my horses, I didn't have to think about anything but the sound of hooves hitting the dirt or the smell of my horse's sweat. As you can imagine, I spent the majority of my free time on a horse; this kind of therapy can't be found in a stranger's office as you pour out your guts. This kind of therapy needs no words, requires no explanation, and is all accepting and all understanding.

. . .

I agree with Buck Brannaman, because during this time I felt worthless, disgusting, degraded – and I was rather mean. Yet every time my little body climbed atop one of these mighty animals, all of that disappeared. These horses were showing me my true worth and value through their own actions and behavior. While I didn't understand it then, I may not have been able to endure that trauma without this truth. Even after the abuse stopped, horses continued to heal my wounds. Even new hardships are eased in my adult life by the many lessons they have taught me along the way, as well as the horses I own today.

Take advantage of these miraculous creatures. They are indeed a gift from heaven.

# Methods of Training

Pressure and Release

The idea here is to apply pressure to your horse until he becomes so uncomfortable he has to move his feet. As soon as he does this, we release the pressure. This creates a reward system for your horse, as well as a process of elimination to figure out what you want from him. There are different levels of pressure for different situations. The rule of thumb here is to start gently and finish gently. Begin lightly, gradually increasing pressure until the feet move. This is a situation where you will have to decide what needs to be done and get it done. Of course, we want it to be easy, but we have to be as firm as required.

To understand what gradually increasing pressure looks like, let's think of rhythm:

.   .   .

*1, 2, 3, 4,*
  *1, 2, 3, 4,*
  *1, 2, 3, 4.*

I think of it like this:

*Light, Medium, Hard, Harder.*

This is called Driving Pressure. A consistent rhythm helps keep your levels of pressure steady, while the horse finds the answer. Deciding how much pressure to use goes back to temperament and bloodlines. You have to learn to read your horse, understand body language, and be able to read the situation. A helpful tip is to remain unemotional when having to increase pressure. What I mean is, we naturally become more aggressive the harder we hit something. Trying to whack something consistently harder and harder, without getting a little angrier, takes some thinking, but we can increase pressure without being aggressive toward the horse. This helps to keep directions black and white.

## SENSITIZING AND DESENSITIZING

Ideally, these two should be well-balanced. Realistically, your horse will need more of one than the other, especially in the beginning, and really depending on breed and temperament. Here is where it really benefits the situation if you know how to help. Whatever happens that day, your end goal should be to help your horse be better tomorrow than he is today, even in the slightest way. Showing your horse he can trust you to give him time to find the answer, or help him find the answer on the ground, will help a riding situation in which you come across a big scary object. The horse already trusts that you will give him enough time to accept the object isn't dangerous, or you will help him feel safe. Putting the time and consistency into these exercises really pays off in the long run.

As soon as I feel my horse tense up a bit and those ears go alert, I know exactly how to handle the situation, allowing me to keep calm and just observe the horse for a reaction. Then I can appropriately move forward with either him concluding there is no threat, or removing ourselves from the situation. Many factors play into the amount of time each one will require. Things like breed, age, environment, and the overall situation of your horse will determine how long this could take. No two horses are the same, so applying this method looks different for everyone.

Sensitize – To cause someone or something to respond to certain stimuli; to make sensitive.

Desensitize – To make less sensitive, or less likely to feel shock or distress.

How do I sensitize my horse? Sometimes horses are stiff or unresponsive to our commands. An example would be an old kid horse. These horses get jerked on, sent mixed signals, and deal with rambunctious kids who are still learning to ride. Because they generally know what to do, a great kid horse will ignore all this and go in the direction the child is looking rather than the direction he is pulling. You can imagine that after some time the horse will be desensitized to the pressure of the bit in his mouth. We can sensitize them to our commands by pointing, acting intensely, and applying pressure.

Let's say your horse is heavy in the mouth. We want to soften this, so we need only a tiny amount of pressure to accomplish the command. Start with your horse on a lead, standing on his left side; your hip should be mid-belly of the horse facing forward. Place your right hand with the lead rope on his withers, with only enough lead to reach the withers. With your left hand, reach down and grab the lead, pulling a little *out*, but primarily *up* towards the withers. You want your horse to 'give you his nose'. When you apply the pressure, as soon as he even slightly gives in to the pressure, release immediately. This needs to be taught to both Lefty and Righty. This exercise will be done until he gives his nose so freely he will reach his nose all the way to touch his shoulder with the lightest pressure.

What does desensitizing my horse look like? First, let's think of a few things our horse would be spooked by. Plastic bags are a big one, a windy day, your hat, your tools, another animal. The list is full of objects in the surrounding environment. Think of any object outside your horse's stall as a potential hazard. The time it takes on each side may not be equal. With the horse on a halter and lead, we will desensitize our horse, using a stick. You should always introduce the object slowly. allow the horse to sniff it; you can rub his nose with it if he allows. If he moves away from the stick, move with your horse, apply the pressure, keeping the object in view until his feet stop. Immediately stop your feet and lower the object, releasing the pressure. Do this until the horse completely relaxes with the object. Next, move to one side or the other, attempting to rub ( apply pressure), until his feet stop moving and he completely relaxes (remove pressure).

As the rule goes, be sure to do the same to the other side. Your horse doesn't learn anything from the applied pressure; he learns that whatever he just did is what you want from him when you remove the pressure.

## APPROACH AND RETREAT

Super simple. Slowly walk up to your horse, reading the body language as you do. If the horse seems uncomfortable or moves away, then you retreat (remove the pressure). Do this until you can easily walk up to him or he comes to you. This is great for building trust and gaining respect.

## BODY LANGUAGE

- Active body language – looking intensely in order to move the horse away from you. This is achieved through sensitization of your commands.
- Passive body language – easing off them and relaxing ourselves, when the horse does as we ask, encourages good behavior such as desensitization, relaxing, standing still, sleeping.
- Ineffective body language – being a pushover, allowing your horse to get away with a few things

here and there. This creates a confused, resentful, disrespectful horse.

- Being forceful – using emotion, anger, or violence to win submission.

You don't want to be the latter. Ideally, you want to be in the sweet spot, which is an appropriate dose of active and passive body language, depending on the situation. Again, this is something you will learn to measure with time and experience.

## RESPECT

Earning respect is essential across the board, no matter the breed, race, or species. You will accomplish nothing without it. Do not skimp on this; it is literally foundational in your horsemanship journey. So how do we gain our horse's respect? First of all, we have to have respect for the animal. This starts with how you care for your animal. Know the spatial and nutritional requirements of your horse. They depend on you to make sure they have a clean space, big enough to move around, as well as food, water, and affection. There is no need for aggressive or violent training methods. The number one way to gain your horse's respect is by moving his feet forward, backward, left, and right. This goes back to the pecking order and nature of your horse. Remember: *whoever moves first loses the Number One spot.* We want to keep the Number One spot as well as gain respect, so we behave like the Number One horse in the herd.

31

# Horse Breeds and Temperament

∿

Six Most Common Breeds

Choosing the right horse will depend on you foremost and what exactly you plan to do with your horse. Different breeds excel at various jobs. You need to take into account your temperament as well as the horse's temperament. You will be partners, possibly for a lifetime; it's imperative you get along with each other. Every horse is an individual, just as every rider has their own unique goals. Breeds are categorized as hot-blooded, warm-blooded, and cold-blooded. If you are a beginner, hot-blooded horses may be too difficult for you to control. In contrast, the cold-blooded horses are slower and more docile – definitely beginner-friendly. Warm-blooded horses tend to be smaller than cold-blooded, and calmer than hot-blooded horses. A well-known warmblood is the gorgeous Tennessee Walker.

Let's take account of the six most common horse breeds:

- American Quarter Horse – Known as the most common breed in America as well as the largest breed registry in the world. This horse is intelligent, athletic, and very versatile. They are generally calm and docile, making them great for families and beginner riders. These beauties' height ranges between 14 and 16 hands.

- Thoroughbred – Most popularly known for horse racing because of their outstanding speed and stamina, they are hot-blooded and tend to be highly-strung animals. They are commonly used in dressage, polo, and jumping. 14 to 16 hands are the average height.
- Arabian – Intelligence, beauty, speed, naturally gentle, and spectacular endurance make an Arabian an excellent choice for beginners who want to participate in pleasure riding, horse shows, and polo. While these horses are considered hot-blooded, they are known to be level-headed. The average height is 15 hands.
- Morgan – These hardy horses can definitely make it through hard times as they don't require tons of feed to maintain a healthy weight. Their bodies are incredibly muscular, with straight, sturdy legs. Easy keepers, I call them. Originating in the US, Morgans are calm, strong, and athletic. Considered coldblooded horses. The average height is between 14 and 16 hands.
- American Paint Horse – these painted ponies are known for their striking spots, power, and athletic ability. Winning in horse racing, western halter, pleasure riding, show jumping, barrel racing – you name it, they can do it! Considered a hot-blooded horse. The average height is between 14.2 and 15.2 hands.

- Tennessee Walker – Our only warmblooded horse on the list, as well as the only gaited horse. The average height is 15 to 16 hands. Tennessee Walkers are walking grace, exceptional trail horses. Due to their calm disposition, they make a good choice for a beginner.

## CHOOSING THE BEST HORSE FOR YOU

You can use this information to help guide you when choosing your horse. I can remember when my best friend decided to buy a horse for her daughter as a therapy tool. I thought this was a great idea, because I know from experience how healing a horse relationship can be. Since they had no prior knowledge or experience, I offered to help them find a good horse for their daughter. They ended up finding someone with a giant 8-year-old paint horse. By the time I arrived with the horse trailer, they had already purchased the horse. As an experienced horseman, I knew right away this horse was inexperienced, flighty – and I noticed he operated in the reactive brain the majority of the time. The seller hopped on the horse and rode him around for about five minutes with no problems, assuring my friends this horse was broke and their daughter would be safe riding him.

I will say selling a horse under dishonest pretense is despicable. This guy knew this horse was intended for a child and took advantage of my friends' ignorance. They didn't ask questions, and just took this man at his word. Nor did they actually ride the horse. Huge mistake. I tried to convince them it was a bad deal, but they loaded the horse up and took him home. If a more experienced person is with you, take their advice. Chances are they know what to look for in a good horse.

In the end, this horse was out of control and dangerous.

Not only that, the money they spent was wasted because the horse couldn't do what he was intended for. They threw more money away with that hefty feed bill, on a horse without a job – a bum horse. It's not the horse's fault. An experienced trainer or rider could have whipped him into shape. The horse also knew the people were new and had no confidence in making him move his feet.

To help you avoid this mistake, I'll share ten tips for buying the right horse:

- Choose a horse suited to your riding goals – what are you trying to achieve with this horse?
- Size matters – you definitely want a horse that is big enough to support your weight without injury to his back. The size is a determining factor when it comes to his job or the event you plan on participating in. For example, you don't want a 14-hand horse to run barrels. It's likely he won't be fast enough for you to place, as most barrel horses are approximately 16 hands and up.
- The right breed – we discussed these above. Choose accordingly.
- Personality – this needs to sync up. You have to like each other. You need to be able to get along and communicate what you need from each other. If you have clashing personalities, it will be a frustrating experience for you both.
- Experience level – make sure whatever level you are at, your horse can accommodate you. If you are a beginner, don't buy a hot-blooded thoroughbred to go trail riding on Sundays. It likely won't work out.
- Ask for help – find an experienced equestrian and ask them to tag along. Take their advice into

consideration when trying different horses. Definitely try out multiple horses before making up your mind.

- Test drive – you would never purchase a car without first test-driving it. I urge you to test-ride the horse on multiple occasions, preferably in different scenery each time.
- Ask for medical records – or take him to a veterinarian yourself. Sellers are not always honest about injuries.
- Ask questions – and more questions. Prepare them in advance, so you don't forget.
- Take your time – I can't stress this enough. Do not rush into a purchase. Horses don't come with receipts for a refund. This should be a slow, thought-out process in which, when it comes down to it, you have all the confidence in the world you have made the right decision.

What are my options for getting a trained horse? You can buy a trained horse. This is rather costly, but convenient. You can train him yourself. This is also costly in time. It can take years to train a horse properly. Lastly, you can pay someone to train it for you. This option is a double whammy. It's going to cost you a pretty penny as well as a generous amount of time. An advantage of training your own horse is you really get to know him. You know what he likes and doesn't like. You find his strengths and weaknesses. You know he has been trained correctly, giving you more confidence in him.

When someone else trains the horse for you, we can never really know how much they have learned or how well they have learned it until you are riding down a trail, the wind blows some leaves around, you get dumped, and your horse is headed back to the trailer without you. My point is there is no guarantee the trainer did enough groundwork, or maybe he rushed through the desensitizing exercises. Now you have to go back and do the work anyway. Doing it yourself really strengthens your bond and ability with your horse.

# General Rules

You can refer back to these general rules that are foundational for the beginner throughout this series. For me, they are reminders as well as motivation. When I'm stuck on a problem, or it feels like I'm lost and just don't know what to do, I come back to these fundamental rules of thumb.

Keep things easy by being as firm as necessary. When I say this, I mean do your research, know your horse, make the required improvements to yourself, so you can train your horse with firmness and confidence. It doesn't have to be frustrating.

Do what you have to to accomplish your goal – a lot of understanding horsemanship comes with time, but if you are willing and able, you are 100% capable. Apply this to your lessons as well. Do what it takes to teach your horse what you want him to know.

Make the right choice easy and the wrong choice hard. Making your horse uncomfortable is a powerful tool. Use it.

Practice makes perfect – this goes for both of you. Cut yourself some slack, You're both starting out not knowing.

That's okay as long as you don't stay there. Keep trying until it's second nature.

Consistency is key – repetitive actions applied with pressure on a consistent basis will ensure you both learn the common language. After repeating the exercise three times, it becomes an ingrained habit. Try starting each exercise three times, three days in a row!

Concept training – use this to teach something for the first time. Don't expect much from the horse; he will be going through his process of elimination to figure out what the correct action is. Don't work on concept and perfection in the same lesson.

Wet saddle pads, long rides, and concentrated training – these are mentioned together because they all play into the same goal. Long rides without wet saddle pads are useless. If you have been on a 3-hour trail ride and your horse comes back without a drop of sweat, that tells me you walked the entire time, and your horse did no actual work. He didn't have to think. The same goes for wet saddle pads without long rides; one without the other is of no benefit. Moreover, concentrated training holds no beneficial effect without both wet saddle pads and long rides.

Pressure and Release – understand this deep in your soul. It's the rock your foundation sits on. Learn it, apply it. Exaggerate it to teach, refine it to keep it.

I wish I had known all of this growing up with my horses. Horsemanship comes naturally to me, so I never thought to research or learn more. Growing up, we had a minimum of 15 solid horses in the barn at a time. My dad was a horse trader, so our barn was a revolving door of top-notch, mostly team-roping horses, but some speed event horses for me. I was able to ride these highly-trained and skilled horses whenever I pleased. This gave me an enormous advantage over any of my peers in competitions. One, I had lots of experience with a wide range of horses. Two, I could ride all of them well.

There is a downside to all of this because it was so easy for me. I didn't really understand how it all worked. I couldn't have told you why this horse behaved this way, and the next behaved another. I also never had to find solutions to any problems. These horses and I could go for hours with no hiccups, but as soon as my brother stepped up, they were a different horse. He even got bucked off a couple of times.

I'm not proud of this, but my dad used to use my riding skills to sell the horses. For example, he would put my li'l 6-year-old self on one of these hot-blooded horses, who were clearly too much for this potential buyer, and have me ride around, gallop, canter, trot, stop, back up, all bareback. He would say, "If that kid can handle that horse, you're golden, ponyboy!"

This is why we never take sellers at their word.

Use the tips I aforementioned to avoid these situations, because this always worked for my dad. Horses don't come with receipts. Once the deal is made, whether the horse adds up to the seller's description or not, he's yours. The point I've been trying to make is that a great horseman does not always translate to a great teacher. While I had horse experience, I had zero 'horse psychology' knowledge, nor did I have ground-work skills.

When I grew up and lost access to these amazing horses, I had to ride average horses, and it was a bit more frustrating for me. I couldn't afford top-notch horses. Neither did I know how to make a top-notch horse. So for years, I struggled to find a horse close to the caliber I was used to that I could afford. To no surprise, I didn't find one.

So I started offering training services to the people at my barn. I had no idea what I was doing, but after some proper time researching and applying what I had learned, along with my natural talent with horses and practice, practice, practice, I knew how to make the horses I couldn't afford.

In the end, I'm so grateful to have lost access to those really high-quality horses. I may have never even thought to understand the process of making such a fantastic horse.

This book is part of a series of horse training books. If you found this helpful, please continue your horsemanship journey with me. My goal is to break the information down into detailed, digestible lessons the reader can really grasp and go out and act on, making it possible to accomplish their horsemanship goals.

# BOOK 2

Round Pen

# Introduction

A round pen is an essential tool in the training process. Horses are very intelligent and are always learning. Whether it's good or bad, they are soaking it up like a sponge. Any time you spend with him on the ground would be considered ground training. If you are unsure of a horse and what they know, or how respectful they really are, the round pen is a perfect place to begin your assessment. Here is where you will establish your place as the leader: *"I am Number One, you are Number Two"*. Working in the round pen can begin as early as they can walk, and deciding where to begin is based on age and stage. This is successful in getting accustomed to each other, establishing leadership, gaining respect, trust and willingness, and introducing the Pressure and Release method.

To begin, you will require simple actions from your horse, but you will require they be done well. Over time, the action requests will become more and more difficult. Doing it this way keeps you from setting him up to fail by asking too much of him. When you are able to move forward safely, the horse is able to develop confidence. One of the main goals in this space is to create a *YES* horse that respects your leadership, and avoid creating a *NO* horse that disrespects your number one position. You don't want the horse constantly fighting you for authority, nor do you want him to avoid you when you are in his view. The round pen is an enclosed space that will give you the ability to control the movement of his feet, ultimately forcing him to focus on you for direction, and increasing his attention span.

Your horse will learn that with you is the best place in this world to be. As soon as you are in view, he will be drawn to you like a magnet. As he learns to respect you as the herd leader, you will be able to establish your personal bubble for safety to avoid being run over, kicked, stomped, or bitten. Ideally, the round pen is the first place you should ask your horse to work, for you to ensure only good habits are formed. Working the lessons in the round pen, the horse will learn to recognize and respond to your body language, move his feet according to the application of Pressure and Release, be willing to engage with you, come to you, follow you, and demonstrate a relaxed form. Through work and rest, you will establish the common language you will rely on throughout the relationship. Good groundwork will translate seamlessly when it comes to riding. These lessons will provide lifelong habits that benefit all – groundwork is not inconsequential. So be patient, and put in the work it takes to develop good ground training. We will discuss how to begin training as well as typical horse and handler mistakes to help you troubleshoot your real-life situation.

You may be wondering what a round pen is. As its name implies, it is a circular pen that can be permanent or portable. Permanent pens are usually made from metal pipe or wooden posts cemented in the ground, where a portable pen is made up of panels, or T- posts and electrical tape. Safety for yourself and the horse is always the number one thing to factor in when choosing your setup. In this book, you will gain the confidence and knowledge you need to do just that and begin training your horse, enabling you to meet your horsemanship goals.

# My Beginnings

When I left home, I hadn't had anything to do with horses for at least five years. All the knowledge I had was what I had gained as a child, riding really amazing horses. At that time I lived and breathed horses. My entire family, as well as my extended family, participated in one rodeo event or another, and we did everything together. One thing I don't remember a whole lot of is groundwork. I think this is mostly because the horses were usually already trained very well. I'm not saying it's okay to exclude groundwork just because they are good horses. It just wasn't a thing for us at this time.

Everything I learned about a horse was from its back. I learned to ride well bareback before I learned to ride with a saddle. This gave me a huge advantage when it came to competing. At a young age I had already learned the value of leg pressure and correct sitting position, as well as weight distribution on his back. I was completely comfortable on a horse. Even after hitting the dirt many times, it didn't turn me away. Horses were my outlet, my passion, and my greatest teacher for the first twelve years of my life.

Then tragedy struck. My parents went through a rather ugly divorce that seemed to break up the entire family and our rodeo adventures together. This was devastating to me as I watched my father sell off all my horses, including my very first love, Cowgirl. Completely heartbroken in all the ways imaginable, my life took a turn for the worst. I no longer had a healthy outlet for my pre-existing trauma or what I was now going through, and turned to drugs, bad choices, and the wrong crowd. To say the least, the loss of my horses was like losing my identity.

Fast forward five years – I'm eighteen and running out of the house. I moved to a town about an hour away. At this point I was pretty heavy into hard drugs. I left with the intention to get clean and start a new life. The first six months were a success as far as getting clean. I bounced around from job to job, though. My older brother moved in with me after I lost my third job as a server. He was a certified farrier and offered me a position as his apprentice. At the beginning of this time, things went really well. He even gave me the first horse I ever owned myself, Anna.

The next six to eight months was a whirlwind of drugs, really hard work under lots of horses, and the beginning of my horse training journey. I share this with you because when all the excitement died down, we hadn't saved even a dollar from all the money we made. Because of heavy drug use, we ended up having a blow out. He moved out and I didn't have a job, nor was I in the position to get one, but the rent was still due. During those six to eight months I was regularly working with my horse, Anna. I kept her at a public horse barn with an arena and round pen on site. It was pretty ghetto, but it was cheap and I could afford it. She was a tri-colored paint with quite an attitude. I tried riding her bareback, with a saddle, in a pen, out of the pen and she was definitely nothing like I was used to riding. I was tired of hitting the ground, so I turned to groundwork in the round pen. She was very smart and had been trained well at one time. I believe that's the only reason I was successful with her, because I had no idea what I was doing.

People noticed the change and how well she was working for me, and started asking me to work with their horses. I always said no, because our shoeing schedule was intense, and I had no extra time or energy. While I had learned a few things about correcting horse behavior being a farrier's apprentice, I still didn't understand the nuts and bolts of the hundreds of horses I ended up under, and I still didn't know what to do or how to start. The fact I had never admitted the true reason ended up working out for me in my desperation to pay rent. I announced on the barn bulletin I would begin taking horses immediately. I took my first horse on for $300 a month. I had no plan, nor could I communicate to the owner what I would even be teaching the horse. Looking back now, this guy was crazy, or just as desperate as I was. Truly, I know my Father in Heaven had his hand in creating this opportunity for me to find my identity again. Long story short – I didn't try to learn anything about lessons in the round pen or how to teach a horse anything, and I failed. The horse was worse off than when he came to me. The owner, for whatever reason, decided to give me another chance, and paid for a second month. I ended up losing my apartment because I couldn't pay the rent, but this just fueled my fire to chase my passion.

I floated around from friends' couches, slept in my car... I even spent a few nights in the stall barn with my horse. I was so embarrassed. I used that second chance money to buy some online courses. I decided once and for all to quit the drugs, and the rest is history. Over time, I learned more and more, people brought more and more horses, and before I knew it, I had created a thriving business for myself.

The ups and downs of my humble beginnings are what have molded me into the horseman I am now. Horses have been a constant saving grace for me. They are more than just an animal – they are part of who I am. My experience is what enabled me to create this series for people to learn things the easy way, rather than having to go through frustration and desperation, leaning on themselves with little to no knowledge.

# Where to Begin

The size of the round pen does matter – 50 feet is the recommended size. Within that is a 10-foot circle you will keep, enabling you to move with your horse. This is also considered your personal bubble, keeping you safely out of kicking range. Inside a pen any bigger than 50 ft, you will struggle to keep up, and find yourself chasing after him. Any smaller, the horse will have a hard time breaking into a canter for you. Your pen should be at least 6 ft high, and the footing needs to be 3-4 inches of sand or soft dirt.

Before you start, be sure to always do a walkaround safety check. On the ground, look for big rocks, holes, or uneven ground. If your pen is permanent and has walls, check that the boards are secure, and there are no nails protruding, or any other sharp objects he may hurt himself on. A quick tip for anyone using T-post and electrical tape is to put tennis balls or aluminum cans over the top of the stakes to avoid the horse impaling himself if he tries to jump over the fence. I mention this because this is a possibility when you begin applying pressure.

Something we have to learn ourselves is how to apply pressure at the appropriate level. Use as much pressure as necessary to get the job done, but as little as possible. You want the horse to respond to subtle cues, to be soft. Rewarding your horse for doing the right action or even attempting to do the right thing is how he will learn the cues. The release of pressure is his reward. By this he uses the process of elimination to find the correct action. Immediate release lets him know he's done right. When you are working closely with him, you can reward him with love scratches and rubs. If he is outside of your bubble, you can use rest and release of pressure.

Something I advise against is the use of treats as a reward in training. It becomes a distraction and can cause them to be pushy or inattentive to you. Treats can be useful to teach him not to run off after removing the halter. By throwing them on the ground he learns to put his head down and hang out for a bit.

Things to consider when beginning round pen training:

- Is your horse hot-blooded or cold-blooded? I ask this because this is vital information we need to approach the horse with the appropriate feel, and pressure. A hot-blooded horse is more likely to require less pressure to get his feet moving because his nature is high spirited, bold, and energetic. They tend to be more flighty and reactive, so you don't want to begin with quick movements and tons of pressure, especially in a new setting. This has potential for a big wreck, like trying to jump out of the pen. A cold-blooded horse's nature is more docile, gentle, and can be lazy. So these guys are more thinkers, less flighty and reactive. These can all be good things, but they can also turn into disrespectful actions. All that extra thinking turns into ideas, to avoid doing any kind of work in every way, meaning they will require more pressure and work on your part to get them to move those hooves.

- Do you understand the psychology of your horse? If you don't know how he thinks or why he does the things he does, you have no basis to begin teaching.
- Is your horse in a healthy mental and physical state? Both of these factors have a bearing on the horses' behavior and ability to perform in the training process. Be sure the horse has had appropriate turn-out time and nutrition before you begin training.
- Do you have a basic understanding of the methods we will be using in this book?
- Pressure and Release
- Sensitizing and Desensitizing
- Approach and Retreat
- Body Language.
- Always start with a warm-up exercise like grooming and rubbing him down all over. This helps desensitize a bit and establish a connection before entering the pen. Ideally you want to be mentally and physically tuned into each other before you start introducing lessons. If the horse already trusts you, he will be more receptive to your teaching and willing to do the actions.
- Results are the indicator to move on or continue the lesson. Time and dates do not provide any benefit when it comes to teaching, as every horse and temperament are different. It may require 5 times, it may require 50 times for him to come to understand the lesson. The only time you should consider is how long you've been in the pen. Too

far upwards of an hour will create frustration and resentment in your horse.

- The lesson should end on a positive note, with the horse doing something he enjoys and does well. This will reinforce his confidence in himself and in you.
- Always, every time, do a cool down before putting him away.

# Assessing the Horse

People being able to approach the horse as well as move around him doing various things is one of the first things we want to accomplish. Your behavior is just as important as the horse's behavior. Move in a manner that is calm and comfortable, so the horse will feel calm and comfortable with you. Especially if this a new horse to you, move slowly and quietly as you begin to assess him. Horses don't communicate with words as we do, so we have to rely on being able to read into their cues by body language. You can refer back to Book One to get an understanding of horse behavior. They can pick up and read our body language, so be sure to keep your calm demeanor to allow the horse to deem you trustworthy. We all have a light and energy that can be either attractive or repelling. He can sense this right away, so keep your manner and outlook bright and positive.

Allowing the horse time to adjust to the setting, especially if he has never been in this pen before now, helps to prevent blow-ups and wrecks. Take a moment for the horse to listen to all the sounds, and smell all the smells, so he can conclude he's not going to die and be able to operate in the thinking brain.

Before I remove the halter, I like to do a few quick exercises to establish my leadership, as well as assess the horse's level of knowledge. Make sure your halter fits, and is on correctly. We will use Direct Feel, which means using physical touch to ask the horse to move. We are using these exercises, not as work, but as a test to see how thorough his basic training is. Later we will use more advanced exercises to troubleshoot problem areas.

In the center of the pen, gently pull down diagonally towards the horse's chest. This will apply steady pressure across the nose and poll. The horse will do one of three things:

- He will give you his nose by giving in to the pressure with a slight tuck in.
- He will hold steady against the pressure.
- Or he will push back against the pressure by throwing his head up.

- Horse No. 1: How willing was the horse to give in? Was it a *big* tuck of the nose or a *little* tuck? Was he stingy, or was he attempting to make the right choice? After a few more times, you need to decide if the horse is being disrespectful, or if he hasn't learned this before.
- Horse No. 2: If this happens, it turns into a game of *whoever moves first loses!* When this happens, I

hold the pressure steady, gradually increasing intensity, until he gives in even the slightest bit. Do it a few times and decide if the horse just didn't know what you wanted, or he's smart enough to ignore your commands and avoid doing work.

- Horse No. 3: Is most likely a hot-blooded horse operating in the reactive brain, but he can also just be testing you by throwing his head up and down to see if you will move your feet first. In his world, if you understand the pecking order, that means if he wins, he's Number One. Horses are very intelligent and learn to do things that can scare beginners, making them think they are Number One in any human-horse relationship. Reading body language can be helpful here to decide if the horse is really uncomfortable with the situation and can't focus on you, or if he is disrespecting your leadership and potentially harming you. If you decide this horse is a threat to your safety inside your 10-ft personal bubble, cautiously remove the lead and move him out, getting those feet moving immediately.

These reactions to applied pressure help us understand the levels of knowledge and respect the horse has. We have to remember how important it is to meet the horse where he's at. Asking too much or too little, without an appropriate amount of applied pressure, can create bad habits that are time-consuming to break.

. . .

Next, I like to ask the horse to back up. First, I will apply pressure by simultaneously wiggling the lead, taking a step towards him, and smooching. If that doesn't work, I will apply the pressure to his nose with that same diagonal line towards his chest, this time more intensely until he steps back. Again you want to ask, how willing was he to move backward? Did he take multiple steps back right away with light pressure, or did you have to keep applying more and more pressure to get one or two steps? After doing this a few more times, you can decide where the horse is at in this area, why he is or isn't responding to your cues, and how much pressure the horse requires to do the action.

Now get back to the center of the pen and stand on the left side of the horse at the shoulder, using your right hand holding the lead rope, and set them up on the wither. With the left hand about halfway between the start of the lead and your right hand, pull a bit *out and up* towards the withers. We are asking the horse to flex and give us his nose by tucking in and bending his neck to this left side. This exercise must be repeated on the right side, and should be repeated multiple times each side. Again, we will make a note of how much pressure he required to respond, and when he did, how willing was he to give in? This should be independently answered on each side. Righty might respond immediately to light pressure, giving generously, while Lefty requires heavy pressure and won't hardly budge, or vice versa.

Last, I like to yield the hindquarters, through indirect feel. This means we will use body language and energy to communicate what we are asking. To begin, your position is at the shoulder facing his hind end, let's say the left side. Like the

59

above exercise, ask your horse to flex his neck, with your left hand gently pulling out and up. You do not need to pull *all the way up* to the withers. Simultaneously, look directly at the hind end with intensity. What you want to see happen is that the left hind leg crosses over the right as the horse pivots on the front left leg, making a small circle. That left shoulder should set up correctly, without him moving too far forward or too close to you. This is a bit advanced, but this is just an assessment to see what level our horse is at. If he responds to this correctly, or even has the slightest idea of how to do this action, I would assume he has been trained at one time or another by someone who knew what they were doing. If the horse has no idea what you are asking, don't worry. We are here to learn the ins and outs of horsemanship.

After this assessment, you should have an idea of:

- how respectful the horse is to your leadership
- what he knows as far as Pressure and Release
- whether the horse is a thinker or more reactive
- is one side worse than the other
- can he back up
- and his willingness to give into pressure.

Wherever your horse is, take note of this to keep track of his progress throughout the lessons.

# The Goal

Gaining respect as the leader in the Number One position is the main goal in the round pen. The horse should immediately give his full attention by showing you his two eyes, responding to your cues, and never giving you his hind end. Gaining his respect is the foundation of your relationship. Just as we learn from the Bible in the book of Mathew 7:24-27, Yeshua (Jesus) tells us to build our house on the steady rock rather than the shifting sand. If you lack respect for each other on the ground, the same will be true when you are riding. Skimping out on this step will be the same as building your house on the shifting unsteady sand, and later on a storm will come to pass and wash the sand right out from under your house, causing it to crumble. This could look like a bad wreck on a flighty horse, a disrespectful horse unwilling to move his feet in the direction you ask, kicking other horses. Really, it is you not having control of the horse or the situation. This is not where we need to be. Build your foundation on the steady rock by following the steps and applying the methods appropriately until you accomplish the goal.

. . .

Our next goal is to establish a common language. This consists of cues, commands, and body language. This language will carry over into riding, giving you common ground and trust, through which you can capture your horse's attention and communicate to him how to handle any situation calmly and safely.

Ultimately, we want to control the movement of his feet – he should move them according to *your* cues or commands. As soon as you point to give direction and smooch to encourage movement, he should be moving those feet. I personally love working in the round pen. I love getting to know my horses, leveling up with them, showing them I care, and respect them as well.

Safety is another reason to begin in the round pen. To assess your horse, you need:

- Enough space to have a personal bubble out of kicking range
- A secure pen to quickly get him away from you
- The ability to control and move his feet if necessary.

*Work*

We will do all the work one step at a time, so nothing becomes overwhelming or too terribly frustrating for either of you. At this point you can remove the halter in the center of the pen. If this is new territory for your horse, smooch him off with light pressure, allowing him to get acquainted with the size of the pen and his surroundings. Your place is the center of the pen in your 10-ft bubble, while the horse is in the outer 50-ft circle. You will need a stick and string, or just a stick, for the following steps:

- Establish Direction

To do this you want to point in the desired direction and smooch, while spanking the ground with the stick and string. This can vary, depending on how much pressure the horse requires to move. You may only need to point and smooch to get him going, or may need to do all three and step towards him to get him moving. Regardless of how much pressure is required, it's best to do these steps at a canter. It may take you some time to get the horse to break into a canter and keep that pace. That's fine. The reason we do it a canter is for the sake of time, trying to get the horse to understand as much as possible in every lesson. No single lesson should last much longer than an hour.

- Change Direction

To do this you have to understand where and what the Driveline is. If you can imagine a string from your belly button to the place on the horse where the cinch goes, in this position you are behind the Driveline. When you move your belly button and string in front of the shoulder, you are in front of the Driveline. In order to change the direction of the horse, you need to step in front of the Driveline, stopping the horse. When you step backwards, encouraging the horse to draw into you, and when he does give you his two eyes, you will now establish direction by pointing and smooching, maybe even spanking the ground as well with the stick in the opposite hand you're pointing with. Now, when he stops, if he doesn't turn in towards you to change directions, you need to immediately cut him off and get him going back in the original direction.

- Draw

To do this, you will stop the horse from moving around the pen by stepping in front of the Driveline, capture his two eyes, and immediately turn and walk away from him, drawing him to you. The goal here is to have the horse follow you around the pen in any direction without losing focus. Stopping should always be your decision. Once your horse is able to relax with you in the center of the pen, be sure to scratch their itchy spots, rub them, show them some love. Establish this center space with you as a positive, rest and reward. Both sides of your horse require this, and this may require you to go back to the working exercises because Lefty spooked at your attempt to rub him. This way we can begin teaching the horse that being in the center of the pen next to you means rest. Eventually they will crave to be with you in the center. This exercise will teach your horse to come right to you, even out in the pasture. Another benefit of this exercise is him following you wherever you go walking or running.

# Common Mistakes

We can all make mistakes, even more so when we are learning something new. Here are some pretty common mistakes we can make as handlers.

- Letting the horse decide when to change directions – our first exercise is to establish direction. Allowing the horse to change direction as he pleases is allowing *him* to be the boss. If this happens, quickly step in front of the Driveline and send him back in the original direction. If your horse is constantly slowing down, trying to stop or change directions, don't ask him to change directions. The movement of his feet must be uninterrupted, and it has to be *your* idea before you ask to change direction.
- Working at any pace but the canter – getting the horse to canter in the beginning may end up being an entire lesson in itself. Especially the cold-blooded, lazier horses. These guys will try every which way to avoid having to do work. It's

important to be sure and let the horse fully commit to his mistake *i.e.,* slow down, before you apply the pressure to speed him back up. Even if you know he's going to break the canter and hit a trot, let him actually do this so he will be able to make the connection between doing the right thing and getting that pressure released from him. Working him in a canter makes the lesson shorter and takes you less time to gain his respect.

- Forgetting to step backward during "Draw" – anytime your horse is moving forward, and you want him to stop or change directions, you need to step in front of that Driveline and immediately take a few steps back in order to release the pressure and draw the horse into you. Without taking the steps backward, you're not removing any pressure, and this confuses him as to what you want. This is especially confusing if you do this sometimes and not every time. Consistency is key.

- Allowing the horse to continue when he turns into the fence – If you don't stop this action immediately, the horse will not know that this is *not* okay. The next time you go to ask him to change direction, he's going to have to guess what the right action is. You must be consistent in what and how you ask.

- Continuously asking – when your horse is moving out, you don't want to chase him around the pen, constantly smooching and whacking the ground. The idea is to ask *once*, using the three steps of cues/pressure. And always allow him to commit to the mistake *before* correction.

- Quitting prematurely – if you stop before the horse is consistently changing directions, did he really learn what you were teaching him? If you or the horse need to take a break, that's completely acceptable. Just be sure to make eye contact with him, getting that respect, before you allow his feet to stop moving. I will repeat myself here, saying the training experience in this pen should always be a positive one. We never want to end in confusion, anger, frustration, or failure to learn at least one thing correctly.

- Unable to stay behind the Driveline – if you find yourself inconsistently behind the Driveline, your horse will not consistently react. What I mean is, if you are in front of the Driveline, asking the horse to move forward, it may come across as him not doing what you are "asking", because he's constantly stopping trying, or trying to change directions – when in reality, your body language is asking him to stop, but your verbal commands are asking him to move forward.

- Pointing in the next direction too soon – you always want the horse to commit to changing directions and giving you his two eyes before you throw up that pointer, ushering him in the new direction. This keeps your timing more precise.

- Sharing the center too soon – before the horse deserves to be in the center with you, he has to be able to consistently change his direction at your command. If you do this too early, the effect will be him turning away from you or not being able to commit to relaxation, making it harder to capture his attention back to you.

- Being overly aggressive – applying too much pressure on your horse will make him feel like he needs to escape you. This contradicts your goal. If your horse feels like you are a threat, I don't imagine he will find comfort and safety in you. This can cause a huge wreck as well. Kicking on fight-or-flight mode in this supposed safe space will inevitably require backtracking.

# Common Horse Problems

∽∿∿⌒

- Turning into the fence rather than the center –
  here you need to be sure you are using this method
  correctly. First step: in front of the Driveline,
  capture his two eyes. Immediately take a few steps
  backward, allowing the horse to draw in towards
  you. When he's facing you directly, switch hands
  and direct him with your pointer in the other
  direction. If the horse will not look at you, the first
  thing you want to do is send him off around the
  pen, and try again multiple times until he gives
  you two eyes. If this still isn't working, but the
  horse is stopping parallel to the fence, and he's not
  giving you his hind end, you can use the fence line
  to walk up to the horse. Use the hand closest to
  the fence to hold your stick and string, and while
  the other hand is pointing, try to push him off the
  fence so that he turns into the center to change
  directions. Now if he is still having trouble, you
  can put a halter and lead on and practice this way
  until it he requires less and less pressure from the

lead to do the action correctly. You can try again without the lead, as long as you aren't too far past an hour of training. You always want to finish on a positive note.

- Allowing the horse to run by – when you ask him to change directions and he decides to run past you, you want to be sure and cut him off immediately. Don't let him take a whole other lap back to you before you get him turned back in the original direction. If he's allowed to continue, he will think that's what you wanted, creating confusion of the common language. It's very important to be consistent with your commands and what you are expecting from the horse each time. If he is consistently attempting to disrupt this, stop asking him to change directions. Let him canter some laps and tire himself out. When you notice he's calmed down a bit or maybe he's starting to lick his lips a bit, try again.

- The horse kicks at you when you ask him to move out – when this occurs, we know this horse is being disrespectful, so we need to act immediately by driving them forward with intense pressure. I would keep this horse moving in the same direction until his body language tells me he's accepted my leadership. Then, because everything has to be done on both sides, I would attempt to have him change directions and work the other side for the same amount of time. Then I would move on to the next step.

- The horse charges you – pay attention to the horse's body language. This is always our warning system. He will always tell you how he feels and what he's doing next. When you see those ears pinned back and he's snorting or kicking up, take immediate action in moving his feet. You need to be intense with the pressure, forcing him to move forward quickly. Remember – *intense* pressure, not *aggressive* pressure. If the horse charges at you, you need to be confident and step forward with your stick or whip – whatever tool you like to use, and whack him as hard as you possibly can across his nose. If you run away from him and leave the round pen, you have created a bad habit, a very dangerous habit. The horse won, he made *your* feet move, he's established himself as Number One. If you are aware this horse charges people and you are not confident in your training skills, *do not attempt to work him.* You could be seriously hurt or even killed, and the horse will go on thinking this behavior is acceptable.

- If the above does happen – you may need to seek the help of a professional horse trainer.
- Running too fast – extra changes in direction. This gets the horse thinking and moving his feet left, right, forward & backward. Allowing this to happen lets the horse think *he's* in control, as well as letting him act like a fool. Majority of the time these horses are the hot-blooded ones. If the horse is real wound up and turns into the fence, it's okay to accept that, until you get him slowed down, using the thinking side of the brain. Once his body language reads he's switched out of reactive brain to thinking brain, you can start asking him to do the actions correctly.
- My horse won't come all the way to me! Not every horse will do this in the beginning. It may take a week for you to gain your confidence in training,

which means it may take you just as long to gain his respect. Don't give up. Keep putting in the work until you get the results you want. Teach him that being on the outside of the pen is really hard work, while the center with you is love and rest. This will ensure your horse willingly draws into you.

- My horse won't follow me! Again, this is a matter of moving those feet with intent. Make sure you are doing the draw correctly, as well as approach and retreat. Give him attention – then take it away. Use his natural curiosity to your advantage. Be sure you are moving in angles and arcs in order to work that hind end, getting those feet crossing and his brain thinking. When you stop moving, attempt to rub his face, then turn away and move forward. Repeat until he's following you everywhere. Another option is a halter or lead: when you walk away and he doesn't follow, give it a tug.

- He turns away when I go to rub his face! Step back and make some racket so as to capture those eyes. Retreat and try again until he relaxes, and you can rub him down without issue. If he leaves the center when you make a little racket, then he has committed to the mistake, and you must send him off to work around the pen. You don't have to make him work too long before you give him another opportunity to do the action correctly.

- Disrespectful behavior – everything boils down to the movement of those feet and how fast or long they need to move. This pressure needs to be applied and removed accordingly and consistently, so there is no confusion as to who is Number

One. When you apply pressure to get your horse to move, be sure to remove the pressure when he does what you ask. Do not continue smooching or spanking the horse, even if you know he's going to slow down. Let the horse commit to the action of breaking the canter and hitting a trot *before* you apply the pressure again.

- Rearing up – this action is an attempt to intimidate you. He wants you to turn away and move your feet. What you need to do is stand your ground and apply pressure intentionally – not aggressive pressure – until he's uncomfortable and stops. This looks like you waving your stick and string at him, whipping the ground and applying intense pressure through your gaze. Rearing up is a lot of work for him. I'd say it won't last long if you handle it appropriately.

- Biting – this is yet another way of him trying to move *your* feet. As soon as he tries this, turn around with the intention of moving *his* feet as quickly as possible. Be assertive! Biting isn't exactly bad behavior, unless he's intending to hurt you, as in drawing blood or picking you up and shaking you. Unfortunately, this happens with horses who been allowed to behave so atrociously by fearful handlers. Nibbling is the horse attempting to move your feet as he would do in his herd to gain rank. Recognizing this puts you in a position to immediately move his feet and win this battle.

- Cutting off the round pen – this is when the horse refuses to stay against the fence the whole way round. He is comfortable with the side he favors, so make that side uncomfortable for him by making him hustle hard on that side, while easing off the pressure on the side he cuts off. Make it hard to be where he wants, and easy to be where he's cutting off the pen.

- Stopping parallel to the fence when changing direction – your first option is to try to capture his eyes and attempt to draw him in, stepping backward. If this doesn't work, that's okay – you have another option. Use the fence to walk up towards the horse's front end with your stick/whip in the hand closest to the fence using your free hand to point in the direction you are asking, all the way up to him if you have to. It's possible you will need to turn his head and smooch him or spank him to move out. If this continues, you need to go back to making his feet move by yielding the hind end.

- In the wrong lead – Left lead, and Right lead. If your horse is traveling to the left, he should be reaching with his left legs in the left lead. If he's traveling to the right he needs to be reaching with his right legs in the right lead. Crossfire is when the front and back ends are traveling on different leads. To correct cross-firing, make them move in a hurry and usually they will correct it themselves. Remember, as soon as the mistake has been corrected, release the pressure to let him know he's done the right thing.

- Trouble catching the horse – the round pen is a starting point, so this is where we will start trying to catch the horse in a smaller space that's easier to control his feet in. If you're having this problem, you need to get the horse to work, moving around the pen at a canter, changing directions consistently. When he's accomplished these, you can try the Draw exercise to teach him being with you is easy and restful. A quick tip: try to spend extra time outside of working with him to practice catching him and drawing him to you so he doesn't relate seeing you to always having to do hard work! Introduce him to the halter and lead rope. Rub him down and scratch him with it. Catch him and take him to graze in another pasture or to the barn and give him a snack. Anything but work!

# Troubleshooting Guidelines

- Before frustration sets in, take a break to evaluate and review the exercise. Ask yourself if you are doing your part correctly. By this you will be able to pinpoint the root problem.

- Return to a simpler action, re-establishing his confidence. Previous exercises he was able to do well many times can bring relaxation and a sense of calm. Returning to simple enables the horse to better understand a more difficult exercise increasing his willingness to learn.

- Practice the exercises he enjoys and is able to do well with ease.

- Return to the difficult exercise, but try a simpler version of it, or at a slower pace.

- After all this you should both be able to return to the original exercise with confidence and positive attitudes.

*Quick tips*

### Do's and Don'ts

- Don't – Don't send your horse away from you aggressively or in a rush.
- Do – When you remove the halter, do it with *patience*, give some rubs even. When you walk away to hang the halter, he will look to you for direction for where he should be in the pen, and possibly follow you around. It's okay to show him you are the best to be in the pen. Then establish your direction with ease.
- Don't – Don't chase your horse around the pen! The fact is, we are prey, and they are predator. Don't act like a predator to your horse, and he won't act like prey around you.
- Do – You do want to create a willing relationship with your horses. Foster his interest and curiosity

in you by walking away from him, drawing him to you.

- Don't – Don't work your horse in a bad mood. Horses are intelligent animals and will pick up on your emotions.

- Do – Do check yourself at the gate, put a smile on your face and remind yourself you can be intense without being aggressive.

- Don't – Don't work your horse into a lather every lesson.

- Do – Do stay close to hour-long lessons, to avoid frustration and resentment.

- Don't – Don't be predictable and boring, doing the same thing every day.

- Do – Do the basic exercises that need to be done every lesson, but then add something new. Make some changes to the routine of the exercises. I'm saying you need to keep their attention and focus on you.

- Don't – Don't skip steps.

- Do – Do follow the steps through every problem that arises with any horse at any age, and you will surely succeed.

# Round Penning a Yearling

Working with young horses is such a pleasure – the beauty of it is starting with a clean slate. If you've had the pleasure of raising your horse from a foal, training can begin from the time he hits the ground. This is so special when a connection or imprint is made from so early on. It's a huge benefit to the training process. If your relationship has just begun at the yearling stage, that's still really awesome and has the potential for a strong mental connection and foundational relationship. Working with horses younger than a year is more about establishing that trust and connection through halter and lead training. Whether your yearling is halter broke or he has never seen a person, we will go through the steps to build a foundational relationship in order to have successful round pen experiences for you both.

# Catching a yearling

This exercise is done in the round pen. You will need a halter and a 15-ft lead, a rope, and your stick and string. You need to use a basic form of approach and retreat to draw the yearling in. The first thing you should do is place your tools down in the center of the pen, keeping the halter with you, and step away. Observe the yearling for curiosity, body language, and willingness. If he starts to look like he wants to approach you, retreat. Allow him to smell your tools and move freely around the pen. You can walk with him at a distance, continuously placing yourself in a position for him to feel comfortable enough to start to approach you, so that you can retreat. The end goal is to draw him into the center with you and get him comfortable enough for you to rub his nose and face. The amount of time this will take depends on his prior knowledge and your relationship. If you've just met, obviously you have to start by gaining trust, and allow him to check out his surroundings, so he knows he's in a safe place with you.

. . .

Your demeanor should be calm, light and positive. You want to be inviting, not closed off or aggressive. Once he's drawn to you in the center, introduce the halter and lead, letting him smell them. Then rub his nose and face with it, and eventually, his neck and back on both sides. At this point you can attempt to halter him. If he runs off, just begin again with approach and retreat. Follow the steps until you have successfully and calmly haltered your yearling. If it has taken you over an hour to accomplish this, take it as a win and stop here. Rub him down with the lead until he has relaxed, then remove the lead.

He will have to stay the night in the round pen and begin again tomorrow. This could take one more day or up to a week. It all boils down to the relationship and mental connection. Once that's made, things will move along much faster and smoother.

Let's go another route and say you weren't able to draw him in with approach and retreat. Your goal now is to get control of his feet. Follow the same steps I mentioned before: establish direction, change direction, and draw. As he is moving around the pen, you are going to get your rope ready and start introducing it nice and slow, with a low gentle swing. Moving too quickly or aggressively can cause him injury, if he's already in fight-or-flight mode.

Now rope him. Once you've got it on, let him continue a lap then step back and pull to the inside of the pen, so he stops and faces you. You can walk around the pen to begin teaching him to give you his two eyes. If you get out of his view and he doesn't follow you with his head, give a tug on the rope until he turns to face you. Then of course reward him with the release of pressure. If he turns to run away from you, quickly pull him back to face you, and release as soon as he does. After a bit of this, start trying to make your way up the rope closer to him, and rub on him as much as you can. If he can relax, go ahead and grab your halter to introduce it, and rub his face and neck down until he has relaxed. Now slowly attempt to put the halter on him.

# Leading

You will need to introduce the Pressure and Release reward system. It's likely your horse will not follow when you pull his lead. He'll probably jerk his head and pull back. Well, even though you have caught him, you don't want to start tugging on the lead right away. Get him moving around you, with a good 10 feet between you. He may be a little flighty, now that he's connected to you, and feeling pressure in new places. It can be overwhelming to take in so much at once. Consider how much of a change this is for him, especially if he came from another place. If he wants to change directions, let him. This is about getting him accustomed to the feel of the halter and lead dangling off his head.

Pay attention to his body language. When you see he has relaxed to the situation, you can move on. This may be a stopping point for you, if it has been over an hour since you began. You want to avoid creating resentment of you or of work in your horse. If this was not a problem for you and you have at 30 minutes left, you can try teaching him to lead.

. . .

You can add some pressure by trying to pull him into you. If he steps in, release the pressure. If he steps back and is pulling on the lead, hold with light, steady pressure until he gives in, even the slightest. Reinforce the reward system – released pressure for attempts and correct actions. Eventually, you will pull and he will take a couple of steps and maybe stop. That's good too. Reward all efforts. Repeat until he gets the idea, and you can lead him around the pen. If you're not able to teach the horse to lead through Pressure and Release, remove the lead and get his feet moving. Go through the steps, and when he meets you in the center of the pen, you can clip your lead back on and try leading again.

# Lunging

For this exercise you will need a halter and lead and the stick and string with a flag tied to it. Your horse should be haltered and standing with you in the center of the pen. With the lead in one hand and the stick in the other, introduce the flag and stick, offering him a smell. Once you've done that, establish direction with the lead hand, using the opposite hand with the stick and flag to apply the appropriate amount of pressure for him to move out into a canter. He may be afraid of the flag. Keep gently waving it until he relaxes about it.

This is the perfect time to release the pressure and ask for a change of direction. Wait to switch your tools from hand to hand until he has committed to the change. Send him off with appropriate pressure from the stick and flag. Again, gently wave the flag until he has relaxed. At this point go ahead and offer rest, by pulling the nose into you. Capture those eyes, and if you have to use your stick and flag, push that hip away and get him facing you. When this happens, release the pressure and allow a minute of rest.

. . .

After this time use the stick and flag to work on some desensitizing. Gently wave the flag left and right in front of his face until he relaxes, then move to one side or the other and wave it by his head until he relaxes, and the same to the opposite side, because we have to look at Lefty and Righty as two different horses. Learning experiences don't always translate to the other side. Then you can touch the horse all over with the flag, until he has relaxed. Always keep your safety in mind when doing these exercises. With green horses, watch the body language, because they can decide their life is in danger at any moment and strike you with front or back legs.

# Flexing

The goal of this exercise is to soften them to pressure and become willing to give us that nose, so later on when you're riding him, he will respond to soft hands and gentle cues from the pressure of the headstall. Standing at the left side shoulder, with your left hand grab the left side nose of the halter. Keep the extra lead rolled up in your right hand and place it on the withers of the horse.

Begin by pulling lightly first, and gradually increasing pressure as needed. You want him to have a bend in his neck and also give you a slight tuck of his nose. Something that usually happens in the beginning is the horse thinks he needs to move his feet and steps backwards as you're pulling his nose in. A common handler mistake in this situation is to release the pressure while he's still moving. Try to keep a bend in the neck while you're waiting for his feet to be still, so when he does stop, he will be in the right position, and you can remove pressure immediately. If this isn't working, he's just not giving his nose, a bend in the neck and he won't keep his feet still, go ahead – use the end of your lead rope to create some pressure to yield the hind quarters. Get that hind end moving, with the legs crossing correctly. Do this for a minute or two. Pull him into a stop, capture the eyes, and try again. Remember – you will have to do this to the other side. You will learn that every day, every exercise is a trial and error. You will soon learn your horse's personality, his likes and dislikes, what he's good at and where he needs the most work. You will be able to time and feel every exercise appropriately and consistently, and trust me when I say, your horse will learn all these things about you too!

# Foal Training

Essentially, every horse, every age can work the steps. The same is true for foals. I like to start establishing a foundational relationship and respect for my Number One position right away. The first thing to tackle is showing them *we are not here to hurt them*. As soon as they are born, we can introduce ourselves and the halter he will wear. Go ahead and rub him down. Show him some love and put his halter on. You can do this for the first couple of days and you always want to do this with Mom around to avoid any stressful situations for Mom or foal.

During these first couple of days really put an effort into gaining his trust, by showing him new things and desensitizing him to the fear of the unknown. He will learn he can trust you in a sticky situation. Truly he will be able to give you more attention if he's not worried about where Mom is. When you feel like he trusts you and has taken interest in your actions, you can start introducing the Pressure and Release reward system to get him moving, and gain control of his front and hind end.

With a simple cotton rope loosely around his neck, you can begin teaching him to yield the hind quarters by holding the rope in one hand and gently nudging him over with your other hand on his hip. Do this on both sides until he understands what his job is. Next you want to show him how to yield the forequarters. Again, you will need a simple cotton rope around the neck as well as his hind end, down around his hocks. The ropes are to help guide him, not to force him to do anything. These two exercises will teach your foal to practice using his thinking brain. This is the start of working that muscle until its so fat reactive brain is overshadowed.

Once your foal has mastered these two steps, you can move to halter and lead training, and then continue on with the steps you've already learned. Just keep in mind they are youngsters, and don't need to be worked too hard or too long, just enough for them to gain some more understanding and respect for you.

# BOOK 3

An in-depth training manual from beginner to professional
Desensitizing, how to spot a relaxed horse, training
techniques, tips, and tricks, flexion, and more!

# Introduction

*"If you surrendered to the air, you could ride it."*
*-Toni Morrison*

Close your eyes and imagine for a second that you were given the task of pulling down a really heavy wall. There is one dilemma though, there is a beautiful rose garden on the other side. Toppling the wall over carelessly, with heavy machinery, could destroy that precious garden of roses behind the wall. Meticulousness becomes your friend in this scenario. Instead of choosing the heavy equipment, you take your chisel and carefully begin to make a dent. Every day, you painstakingly chip off each piece of brick. It stretches out your patience, your time, and the muscles of your hands, but you don't give up because you have the rose garden in your mind. You hammer, scrape and pull, but the wall only seems to get taller. It mounts over you like a threat until eventually, one day, you begin to make headway. Each day after that initial headway making day things get easier and you begin to see progress, until one day you are standing and looking into the beautiful rose garden on the other side.

Horse training is much like the parable shown above. It can be a difficult task and a long road to walk. It requires patience, time spent on your feet, and learning and unlearning the antics of your horse. Like the huge wall, it is easy to get lost in the idea that you haven't made any progress. However, remember that while it may seem like you are going in circles, you may just be walking up a spiral staircase and making progress towards your goals with every step. But, what if I told you there was a way to break down that wall with ease?

In the summer of 2019, Kevin Babington an Olympian show jumper and trainer suffered a life-changing accident at the Hampton Classic. Kevin and his horse Shorapure were jumping 5 feet in the air, flying over the jumps, and proceeding through the course, when he was thrown from his horse. He landed headfirst which resulted in bruising his spinal cord, leaving him paralyzed from the chest down. You would think that after an accident like that you would step away from the sport. He believes that not only will he regain control of his body and walk, he will even ride once more. Kevin has been known to say that the greatest thing he has learned on his road to recovery is that he has learned what patience really means. Little by little, miraculously, his body has begun to heal.

When riding a horse with a strong will, accidents are bound to occur, even for skilled athletes, but Kevin was confident in his abilities. Despite having broken his shoulders, collar bones, fingers, and nose, and once separating his pelvis, Kevin was infamous for showjumping without protection. However, that year at the Hampton Classic, things changed. What happened to cause this incident? Kevin's mare jumped too soon because of a shadow and ended up crashing.

Although Kevin is now recovering from his injuries and he continues to coach from his wheelchair, he does not compete anymore. This shows that even for competitive horses and highly trained and seasoned riders that have won numerous titles, training and reaffirming the fundamentals of horsemanship is necessary. You never know what may happen.

The first chapter of this book focuses on desensitizing your horse. Horses have an inclination to be flighty and spooked by random objects. This could be things as harmless as a plastic bag flying in the wind, a trash can, another animal, or a fellow horse galloping at full speed. Decreasing sensitivity to non-harmful stimuli makes for a bold, confident horse that adheres to instructions no matter what happens. This is also referred to as "bombproofing," your horse.

In chapters one and two of this horse training series, we explored the horse's psychology, and nutrition, and establish the fundamentals of gaining the trust of your horse. The ability to surrender your previous biases, impatience, and fear is key to mastering your horse. In this book, I will guide you step-by-step on how to desensitize your horse, how to carry out disengaging and yielding, and the importance of backing up. These are technical procedures that have to be done with minimal mistakes. This is the main reason why practice guides are implemented after each lesson. Every chapter is tailored to the needs of each reader, whether you are a beginner, intermediate, or experienced horse trainer looking to get new perspectives into proven training techniques garnered over an accumulated 20 years of riding, training, and management experience with horses. I spent 10 years attending clinics, polishing my knowledge, and teaching others. I have written this book so that you don't need to spend that cumulative 30 years in order to learn how to train your horse. This book contains distilled knowledge of horse training, handling, and mannerism, and all of my expertise is designed to help you on your journey to become a successful, knowledgeable equestrian.

The journey of horse training is one that you really need to surrender to. Do not regard it as combat, even while it may at times largely involve asserting your dominance. While breaking down your wall, I can show you vulnerable spots in the wall that would make the defense lowering process faster and easier. In this book, you will gain the ability to desensitize, disengage, and backup your horse in a safe, practical, and well-guided manner. If you're ready, follow along with me while I guide you along your journey to great horsemanship methods.

## Desensitizing

Years ago, I trained a horse named Bailey. She was a beautiful black mustang. She had a graceful stride and a fiery countenance. When I rode her, I understood the definition of being on a high horse like I never had before. She inspired confidence and cantered without a care in the world. But, with all her beauty, grace, and potential, Bailey had a problem. Her previous owners had not properly desensitized her. As you can imagine, this created havoc with everything this mare did. She was unsure, and spooked frequently, leaving little to be trusted with her.

In book one of this series, we discussed the different horse breeds categorized into hot-blooded, warm-blooded, and cold-blooded. Bailey was a hot-blooded mustang that operated mainly from the reactive side of her brain. This means that she had the potential to be hazardous and untrustworthy since she was not adequately desensitized. She could be feral sometimes and downright snobbish. Her beauty matched her attitude. Despite this, Bailey was a lovable horse, and she knew how to move her hooves. After I began working with her, we had already established a sense of trust and familiarity, and it would have been a considerable loss to let her go. I had to work on desensitizing her to make her the best version of herself.

In book one, we also gave a little background to desensitizing and how it differs from sensitizing. At the same time, sensitizing involves causing your horse to respond to certain stimuli; desensitizing means: "to make less sensitive." A balance should be achieved between these two concepts.

Desensitizing is eliminating your horse's flighty response to certain stimuli. The stimuli could come in the form of a loud, sound, sudden movement, other animals, or who knows what you may face. This is done in a controlled environment to prepare the horse for success. Note that there is a difference between desensitizing your horse and building confidence. In desensitizing, you want them to remain calm in the face of unfamiliar things that poses no actual threat. On the other hand, building confidence involves making our horse yield to specific tools like a stick and a flag and respecting that instruction.

TOOLS FOR DESENSITIZING

Before picking out a tool, remember to introduce it to the horse. Let it smell the device and feel it around its body. Horses are prey animals whose instincts are tailored to self-preservation. We are working with the horse, not against the horse, so always remember that this is a learning process for them.

### 1. **An old feed bag**

This simple, low-cost, easily sourced item elicits good results. If there is no feed bag, a small tarp is a good alternative. When you get the feed bag, wad up the tip, ensuring to leave a little air in the bag. Hold your horse steadily by the rope, and begin to shake the bag. Shake the bag until your horse begins to show signs of relaxation, then take the pressure away. One advantage of the feedbag is that it makes a lot of noise. Expect your horse to get nervous the first time you try this. For easily spooked horses, you want to achieve relaxation from them before they get to be still. It is best to withdraw when they show even the slightest bit of peace.

Remember that whatever you do on the right-hand side, you must also do for the left-hand side. Engage not only their sense of hearing but their sense of touch. Next, touch them with the bag. Again, repeat this on the left side and right side, and apply some pressure until the horse relaxes.

When carrying out this exercise, stand your ground and be confident. Horses can sense energy. They will be tuned into or repelled by these energies we emit. They know when we are nervous or scared, and that vibration can be soaked up and exaggerated by them. Of course, we do not want to do anything that would hurt our horses but introducing that element of discomfort while desensitizing can present much more harm than you realize, and it may prevent them from coming to you and in turn prevent a true relationship from being developed. Underexposing them would appear as tiptoeing around them, making a little noise with the feedbag, stroking them lightly, and approaching the exercise as though you are walking on eggshells. Remember that this is for their benefit and yours in the long run.

1. **A lariat rope**

This tool requires a little more handiness than the feedbag. However, you can substitute it with any rope. You can swing the lariat or a string in the air, or make noises with it. One of the most effective ways to use it is to put it on them. Get them comfortable with it. Make a loop with the rope and place it on the horse's hindquarters. Once they get relaxed enough, you can tighten the cord and allow them to step into it with their hind leg or forefeet, above the hock, or around the belly. This gets them used to the sensation of a saddle.

1. **An Australian stockwhip**

The primary use of this tool is to get the horse used to sudden noises. A whistle, a sudden clap, or metal scraping against the floor. Simple things like these can get your horse to become spooked easily. We don't want that happening because no matter how controlled the environment is, noises like that are bound to occur.

Grab your whip and hit it on the floor on the left or right side, depending on which you choose. Make the noise consistent and look the horse in the eyes as you whip. Continue until the horse shows a little bit of relaxation. It can be as simple as staying still or not tensing up. You can apply a pattern to the exercise. First, swing the rope around, then snap it. As they get more comfortable, you can begin to move around with the rope.

1. **The Stick and String**

This consists of a string and a stick which you would use as an extension of your arm. Like the lariat rope, use it all over your horse's body- the rump, wither, neck. If the horse moves away, keep with the pattern until the horse relaxes. Next, begin waving your string at a 90-degree angle with your body turned away from him in order to show you are not a threat. Slowly move closer to him. If he moves, keep with the pattern. If you stop when he moves, you are rewarding incorrect behavior, and the purpose of the training is defeated, so stay with your horse. You are in control of this process, this can be an easily forgotten idea, but it is necessary for properly training your horse.

## SIGNS OF A RELAXED HORSE

One of the critical points in desensitizing is immediately removing the pressure when your horse relaxes. You need to learn to release pressure and create a reward for your horse, so they know when they have done something correctly. There is an unwritten language between horse and ride. You may be asking, "How do I know for sure if my horse is truly relaxed?"

1. *They may take a deep breath.*
2. *Shifting their weight to indicate they are comfortable standing there*
3. *A low-head carriage*
4. *Their nose is tipped in and inclined towards you*

5. *Licking and chewing*
6. *Cocking a hindfoot and resting it*

Some horses may soften their eyes. There is the absence of the big bright shiny eyes they may have when nervous. If you learn to pay attention and hone in on these soft cues, you will give yourself a huge leg-up in the training and desensitizing process. Understanding your horse's body language is key to effective training.

## TIPS FOR DESENSITIZING YOUR HORSE

1. *Apply the pressure consistently and take the strain of stress away at the right time. Keep a rhythm to the movement of your desensitizing tool.*
2. *Relax. While desensitizing, take a deep breath to reassure your horse that all is safe.*
3. *Make a little progress every day.*

*Be patient enough to know how to recognize the slightest hint of relaxation, then release pressure. Your horse may not take a day to get desensitized, and that's okay.*

Now the question on your mind could be, "what if my horse is spooky or wild? Are all these steps foolproof?"

I will answer by telling you the story of Buck. Buck was a fretful horse that was scared of everything. I learned from him that no two horses would behave the same. I used to have a theory for desensitizing horses, and I had assumed that a well-thought-out plan would work for all the horses I came across. Buck shattered that thought process I was currently in. When I tried to put the desensitizing tool on his body, he moved around in wild circles, and keeping him steady was a lot of work. The exercise was always a test of my courage to stand firm and remain number one. However, things changed when I included a straightforward tweak to the desensitizing routine.

I let him *follow* the object.

This worked because the object was moving away from him as I lead him with the rope. You are "tricking," the horse into thinking that they are chasing it, which builds their confidence. Instead of you imposing the object on them.

Next, I introduced noise-making with the feed bag; this time, I used it at a distance from him. As he got comfortable, I reduced the intensity and inched closer. Of course, he reacted to this. Now, in this situation, I held firm. The safest position is with your body at an angle to the horse's shoulder, and your hand up by his eyes. Desensitizing a wild horse takes a lot more work. Be prepared to move around the round pen and expect a lot of dust to be kicked up. I kept at it until his feet stopped moving. Even then, I did not take away the pressure. Why? Because I realized in the past that he sometimes faked it.

Buck came around eventually, and what I once thought of as an impossible situation became something I could handle.

Do not retreat early. And remember to reassure the horses when they get it right.

Here's a popular question I get from my years of practice. "How do you get a rope on a horse that has never been roped on?"

First, you need a round pen. You may get away with using a square pen enclosure, but anything too big could pose a lot of trouble for you. Use an old, soft rope, so you don't burn or wound your horse. Start with the rope's end, roll about six coils, and cut the pen in half.

1. *Throw the rope on the horse from the back end.*
2. *You will get exhausted moving around the pen, so cut it halfway from the horse in each direction and keep switching eyes.*
3. *Try to throw the rope behind the withers. The string gets carried a few steps before they shrug it off their bodies.*
4. *You can add a coil when they begin getting used to the roping.*
5. *Ensure you never rope at the gate of the pen. Wait till the horse gets past it.*

**Pay attention.** If the horse turns towards you, take the pressure off.

1. *Once you get the rope around to a large extent, draw the horse towards you in a firm manner.*
2. *You will see that the horse is slowly getting accustomed to the rope. Take it off and put it back on. Rinse and repeat.*
3. *Once you can get the rope around the horse, you can practice getting the rope around its feet.*

Once you get the horse comfortable with roping, you can put the halter on.

## GETTING THE SADDLE ON

Simply put, you have to desensitize your horse correctly before getting a saddle on. When you get the harness on, you want to get it right. You don't want it slipping off underneath the horse or tearing up. You generally want to ensure the first experience is uneventful. If your saddle gets underneath the horse, he gets misinformed and thinks that if he bucks around, the harness comes off. The first few experiences lay the foundation of how the horse reacts to saddles afterward, so we must do it right. And, of course, we do not want to go racking up repair bills on just the first try. You may want to practice with a quieter horse before moving to your horse that has never been saddled.

1. *Rub the horse and get some feels in*
2. *Put the rope around the horse and hold it still*
3. *If the horse moves, hang in there till he becomes quiet*

107

4.  *Repeat the desensitizing steps done with a flag and stick*

5.  *An ideal beginner saddle pad has a hole that you can stick your hands through like a mitten. This makes the work more manageable, and you can pet him with it. The aim is to get him comfortable with the saddle pad before the real deal comes in.*

6.  *In the previous books in this series, we mentioned how most horses are more comfortable on the left side. You may want to practice saddling from the right side. Any action done on the right helps the horse learn better. It is much like doing a difficult task to build the resilience and confidence of the horse.*

7.  *When it's time to pull the cinch up, do NOT bend in a way that puts the crown of your head in his kicking range. Instead, reach down with the back of your hand touching his belly.*

The pressure and release method applies to the cinch too. You have to tighten and release a few times. This is because the first time it is pulled up, the pressure and release make them realize that this isn't an activity that hurts or one to be afraid of. Often, if a horse is going to buck right as they disengage with a saddle on, it will cut loose.

In the following few chapters, we will expand on yielding and disengagement.

. . .

## GETTING A HORSE CONFIDENT WITH A BULLWHIP

This is similar to what you do with a rope. Start at a distance and gradually work your way closer. Let the horse get a feel of it around its body. Add a little bit of noise and pop while walking in an arc and leading with the rope. Gradually increase the number of pops until the horse relaxes.

## DESENSITIZING A YEARLING TO A CRACKING WHIP

A yearling is a young horse between one to two years old. Yearlings are almost always fully weaned and independent of their mothers. They are not yet ready for riding as their joints are still maturing and susceptible to overwork. A yearling can be lunged, round penned, and should be cooperative when being loaded into a trailer.

People may object, but research is quickly showing that establishing trust with your horse does the work of desensitizing much easier. You want to put them in a position where they are rock-solid in the knowledge that nothing you do will hurt them. The connection is the foundation you establish before laying other pieces of training on top. By the time you begin desensitizing with the cracking whip, the horse will not respond erratically.

· · ·

Dr. Stephen Porges developed the Poly Vagal theory in 1994. His theory is essentially a collection of unproven evolutionary and psychological constructs that involve the vagus nerve's role in emotional regulation, social connection, and fear response. Although it was first applied to humans, we can see how this extends into the behavioral pattern of horses.

### *"How does it work?"*

The mind and body are connected through the vagus nerve, stretching from the brainstem to the colon. The vagus nerve helps to regulate heart rate, digestion, speaking, and other vital aspects of being alive. As we take in information, the vagus nerve helps control it. Think of an emotionally devastating time in your life. How did that period affect your ability to learn, communicate, and focus? Although it differs from person to person, most of the time, having a shaky emotional core affects our cognition. Horses are no different. We speak the same language that transcends verbal cues. When we are adequately nurtured, it increases our capacity to grow. Sometimes, that seemingly obnoxious yearling might need a little bit of love.

*Sensitizing*

SENSITIZING

We have said a lot about desensitizing, but it must be balanced with sensitizing, which we defined earlier and brushed on in book 2 of this series. When we are sensitizing our horses, we want them to get used to specific cues that we want them to respond to. For example, pointing in a direction and clucking could be your signal for the horse to move in that direction. What you want to do is to get him accustomed to that stimulus.

When riding, you want to get the horse to respond to movements you make with your legs. One such example is to move its hip by putting your leg around where the back cinch goes. As previously mentioned, sensitizing differs from desensitizing.

In book one, we established the importance of a round pen. We will go over that again to say that the round pen is a circular space that gives you the freedom to be in control of the horse's movement. A round pen allows the horses to run around the pen. This means that it is not in your best interest to chase the horse. It is essential as a controlled area to do ground training and exercises such as sensitizing.

CUES FOR HORSE RIDING

Cues are signals given to a horse when we expect them to behave differently. They can either be shown on the ground or on the saddle. They are a significant part of training and communicating with your horse.

"How Do You Use a Cue?"

If you are on the ground, when communicating cues on the ground, we can either use your voice or body language to cue the horse. For example, teaching your horse that they ought to back up when you raise your hand is a cue. If they do not respond immediately, add more energy to the cue until they relax.

Then, reward the behavior and repeat the cue.

To cue a horse under saddle, we would be using our seat, hands, legs, and sometimes our voice. Like we do on the ground, we would also apply the pressure and release method. A few more examples of cues are:

1. *Cueing your horse to lay down. You can do this by tapping the ground with a dressage whip.*
2. *Teaching your horse a Spanish walk; can be achieved by lifting your whip in front of him*
3. *On the saddle, you can cue your horse to break into a canter by putting your outside leg backward*
4. *Close your right leg to turn him left and vice versa*

An act as simple as picking the reins and shifting your weight can cue your horse to get ready for movement. Moving your weight to the back can be a cue for the halt.

This is just a simple illustration of what a cue can look like. You are free to explore other cues that work with your horse. Cues can also be subtle. For example, if you come into the barn after a stressful day and your face is tense and tight, your horse can sense that and react by moving to the back of the barn. That expression on our faces has served as a cue without our knowledge.

There is a story of a horse named Clever Hans. Clever was said to be a horse with such a high intellectual capacity; he could do arithmetic problems and count. But, of course, this wasn't entirely true. What Clever did was that he read cues from his owner. When he got close to the correct answer, he would watch and pick up the change in the expression of his owner.

Humans do the same, not surprisingly.

It was studied by John Gottman and Paul Ekmann, and they came up with proven research to show that micro-movement and expressions in humans translate into our behaviors and feelings around other people. In summary, cues can be obvious or non-obvious, and exploring them with our horses is an excellent way to build familiarity.

# Disengaging and Yielding

A horse who has been taught to disengage or yield has been trained to surrender, relax, and submit. This is an essential exercise as a disengaged horse cannot buck, kick, or bolt.

Disengaging the hindquarters is an important tool to have in your arsenal as it teaches young horses to back away from pressure, and it is often advisable to start preparing your horse for this from a young age. It also comes in handy for other activities like getting your horse to be in motion when working on the lunge and riding them on a saddle. When things are starting to get out of control, it is essential to have a method to calm them down and get them grounded and safe.

### *"What does it mean for a horse to be disengaged?"*

When a horse is disengaged, the earliest sign is that their back legs are crossed. To practicalize it, try crossing your legs while standing. Then, get someone trusted to shove you slightly from behind. You will see how secure you are and less likely to stumble. Now, try to do this with your feet apart. You will notice that the balance is missing, and you will be unable to brace against the impact of that push. The same goes for the horses when they are disengaged.

In this position, they are locked, secured, and steady. They are unable to rear up or kick or perform dangerous maneuvers suddenly. So when we teach them to disengage their hindquarters, we reaffirm our position as number one and disable them from performing behaviors set against the grain of what we want to see.

As with other exercises, we want first horses to be comfortable with the stick. We want them to know that it is just an extension of our arm and nothing to be fearful of. As we mentioned earlier during the desensitizing section, your body language should be relaxed and confident.

Next, you have to instruct and slightly move the inside hind foot underneath their body with your stick. This is why desensitizing is a vital ground training that every horse must undergo.

Imagine a situation where a horse who has not been appropriately desensitized is introduced to this process? He would get spooked and leave you hanging, or it would quickly escalate into a dangerous affair. Depending on the age and stamina of your horse, the distance of the hindfoot may change.

. . .

The hindfoot you are working closest to must step up underneath their body and not behind. For example, if you are working your stick towards them from the left, the left hind foot should be moved. Keep in mind the concept we spoke of previously of the left-hand and right-hand sides.

### *"What Happens if my Horse is Too Spooky for this Method?"*

For cases like this, it is best to approach it patiently. Start with a bit of desensitizing, rubbing down the horse with the stick while holding on to the rope with your other arm. Keep your position steady and lean slightly towards the direction of your stick to let the horse be very much aware of your presence. Rub the horse with the stick and tap somewhat on the hip where you want the horse to move. A lot of trial and error may occur in this process. What mostly happens is that the horse brings that foot backward instead of forwards as we want it to.

Rub to reward the horse to let them know taking a step was the right thing to do. Remember that to get the optimal behavior from your horse. You have to keep the principle of pressure and release at the back of your mind.

A second method of teaching your horse how to disengage is to lead with the rope. This method differs from using a stick and is considerably less stressful for some trainers. You take the string and try to get its nose to connect with its rear end. Of course, this is physically impossible. We want to lead with the rope, and subsequently, the horse begins to step with his hindquarters over while staying straight. Try it on both sides and notice how the horse keeps slacking the rope instead of leaning on you.

### *"What Happens if My Horse Keeps Leaning On Me?"*

When this happens, you could take the rope up, keep the section closest to the horse a little straight, and bump the nose away with a tug. Now, this is applied pressure, and you want to reward your horse when he gets the movement right. Overall, we want to start by ensuring the horse receives some steps. It does not necessarily have to transition into a full circle with its hind legs.

### *"What if My Horse Just Bends Their Head Around and Doesn't Move?"*

In this case, you will have to combine the rope's movement and tapping the hindquarters to let the horse know he ought to move it. If the horse has a saddle on, keep your rope in the same direction as before and give it a tap on the strip.

Teaching your horse to disengage is a core exercise for a groundworker. You want to keep your horse upright, steady, balanced, and on all four quarters. You want to keep the halter rope slack, and if there is any bending or leaning from the horse, remember to tug very slightly.

SHOULD YOU TEACH DISENGAGING TO YOUR HORSE OR NOT?

. . .

Many unconventional opinions abound surrounding whether you should teach your horse disengagement or not. There has been a lot of discussion surrounding the topic for some years. This book commonly teaches your horse to disengage its hindquarters in horsemanship clinics and elsewhere. However, while it has obvious advantages, some people believe this thought process is something that should be avoided entirely. Now, because I am transparent in writing this book, and my sole aim is to ensure the delivery of quality horse training, I will be stating the proposed cons of teaching your horse to disengage.

One of the reasons is that when we are disengaging the horse's hindquarters, we take their hind leg well beyond their center of balance. You might ask, "so what happens then?" The story doesn't end with you disrupting their center of credit, and it is also said that when this happens, you are hyper-flexing the horse's joints and overstretching the muscles in the hindquarters. The inside hind leg and outside shoulder are the primary sources of the horse's balance. When you take that inside hind leg beyond the center of balance, the horse is shoved onto its forehand. Eventually, this is said to cause problems like lameness in the horse's front end. Horse's are creatures of habit, and teaching them to disengage frequently makes them learn by default to bear too much weight on their forehand. This predisposes the horse to issues with lameness and transitions. There is also the risk of back tension, distress, and high tension muscular issues caused by stretching. The horse may also struggle with collection due to bearing too much weight on the forehand.

. . .

However, this should not scare you or stop you from teaching your horse how to disengage. Teaching disengagement is as important as installing brakes in your car. I once had an experience of being dragged over a hundred meters by a horse that refused to stop. Teaching disengagement has saved many lives. What you should be careful of is repeating the process too frequently. Once they have learned it, avoid repetitive pressure. Alternatively, some horse trainers carry out some forward flexion exercises before disengagement.

Of course, some people do not believe this thought process about avoiding disengaging. The hindquarter stance on the issue is that although disengaging is essential, it should not be overdone.

## YIELDING HINDQUARTERS AND FOREQUARTERS

In 1986, there was a nuclear explosion in Chornobyl. It left Swathes of Ukraine and neighboring areas of Belarus contaminated. People died from radiation poisoning and its long-term effects, such as cancers. A no man's land was created within a 19-mile radius from the explosion site. Scientists and researchers proposed that the area would not be fit to live in for another 24,000 years.

However, 35 years after the disaster, a swarm of rare animals has taken over the area, particularly a breed of wild horses native to Asia called Przewalski's horse. Although some animals were introduced into the ecosystem, the wild horse showed extraordinary survival abilities and thrived beautifully even in a place filled with the haunting ghosts of destruction.

. . .

Horses, although prey animals, can show a degree of resilience, although this is also dependent on the type of breed. As mentioned in book one of this series, what we want to achieve is the best out of our horses, which involves training them to maximize their temperament. It dictates how careful we ought to be while training, the level of pressure we have to add, and the release time. Some horses, although resilient, also have a great deal of ego and will. Disengaging and yielding is an excellent way to teach the horses to submit.

Yielding hindquarter is an integral part of disengaging the horses' hindquarters. Horses are impulsion animals with a lot of natural impulse that stems from behind. You can think of the horses' behind as the gas pedal and the front as the steering. We have previously referred to disengaging as a brake you apply in emergency cases. In yielding, what we want to achieve is a state where we can simply point at the horses' bottom, and they move it out of your space.

Remember that a base down your eye line is a sign of disrespect. What I do is, when I teach my horse to stop, I pick up a lead rope and urge them to swing that hind leg around. I point at the bottom and move that bottom one step at a time. I use my stick to add pressure and keep myself at a safe distance.

As stated before, we begin working on the hindquarters by leaning in. Let your body language be full of intent. Then, start to amp on the horse's hip. Amp means applied measure of pressure in this case. Remember to be patient with them. Release pressure as soon as there is movement. Tap rhythmically on the hips if possible, as consistency aids in applying pressure. Count;

. . .

*One Two Three*
  *One Two Three*
  *One Two Three*


Keep it steady until the horse moves, and then reward the horse with a rub on the withers.


## YIELDING FOREQUARTERS

Yielding forequarters translates as four things mainly.


1. *A turn on the forehand*
2. *Laterals*
3. *Side passes*
4. *Half passes*


This helps the horse to reconnect their brain with its forefeet. When I teach a horse to yield its forequarters, I typically prefer to practice against the wall or the fence. This prevents the horse from moving forward because, naturally, your instructions will first be perceived as annoying stimuli that they wish to move away from, and our intent is for the horse to cross.


Sometimes horses are afraid of the wall, as with most other things. This is okay; give our horse some time to come around and some rubs to reassure them that all is fine. It is natural for a horse to feel claustrophobic, and the wall can make them feel trapped.

. . .

## Lateral leg yielding and half passing

The lateral leg yield is a movement in which the horse travels simultaneously forwards and sideways. The horse is supposed to be straight and steady with his body in this movement, but while maintaining a slight bend is to be noted in the direction of travel. The leg yield is one of the first lateral exercises inculcated into the horse's psyche. It is a simple lesson that teaches the horse how to move sideways away from leg pressure.

One of the most popular places to practice a leg yield is from a rail to a quarter line. Another way is to practice it with the nose of the horse in front of the fence. Another alternative is with the shoulders or haunches to the wall. Remember to keep the body of the horse parallel to the wall.

The lateral or leg yield differs from the half pass, although they are often confused because the horse moves straight ahead and sideways. However, the half pass is more advanced and demands a high balance, collection, and engagement from the horse. Collection means that the horse's center of gravity is shifted backward. The energy is directed in a horizontal direction with reduced forward movement.

## Additional elements of groundwork

Another element of groundwork is the turn on the hindquarters, and it is used to change directions while working on the ground. One thing to note is that the horse is heavy on the forehand as they carry two-thirds of their weight on it, so if we want them stepping the shoulder around, we want to get them to throw the weight off that shoulder, and we want to rock some of that weigh backward.

This works best after you have established an excellent lateral flexion, and we want them responsive to the direct feel: the halter or hackamore on the neck. Also, we want them to respond to our indirect feeling, the position we take, and our body language. We can do this in isolation from a standstill. Using the rope, we get some movement by bringing the shoulder towards us and sending it around.

*Rinse and repeat.*

This exercise aims to keep their weight on the back foot. Next, we want to apply this while mounted on the horse. The essence of groundwork is to help find a translation and appropriate use when we ride eventually. In that position, continue as before, using the rope to lightly put the weight off the shoulders. Rock backward with your weight and step away from the legs, so the outside leg in the first position is what steps the shoulder across, reaching our leg ahead in the first position. Do not over flex your horse laterally here. The primary key is to get some weight off the shoulder.

The element above is essential when teaching our horse to side pass. Training a horse to side pass has a lot of advantages ranging from groundwork improvement to enabling you to open the gate of the pen while seated on the saddle. After properly desensitizing, you have to train your horse to turn on a backside.

When the horse is relaxed, then we proceed. To ask the horse to move the inside front foot across, put your fingers where your foot would be at the girth when riding, then take your hand and put it up towards the horse's eye. This move is to help support the horse in crossing over. You also want to step in front of the horse to help her cross the front foot. You also want to be making a move towards the eye, and if the horse still doesn't move off, take the heel of your hand and slightly bump down on the cheekbone for extra support. Eventually, all these signals culminate in the horse's brain, responding to the sensation of your finger on the girth, finally moving forward. As the horse moves, release pressure and offer a reward to let the horse know it has made the right choice.

Sometimes, leg yield is taught to the horse alongside a turn on the forehand, and a turn on the haunches. I like to begin with groundwork training as it teaches the horse how to handle leg pressure.

Firstly, visualize where your leg hangs while riding your horse. Yes, it is the girth area. What we do is move our legs back, to move the hindquarters over. To simulate that feel on the ground, we have to use our hands as previously explained for the leg yield. Steady the horse's head with our other hand without constantly touching it. The reason for guiding the head is to correct the course of movement when the horse seeks to move away from the source of pressure. We want to guide them in the direction we want instead. The net thing to do is to apply a bit of pressure with the hand on the girth. On a hot-blooded horse, apply a little pressure, stop and reward when they move.

### *"What if My Horse Doesn't Move at All?"*

I trained a horse named Timothy over 5 years ago. He was the direct opposite of Bailey. He was cool to a fault. This meant that he was unafraid, but it also translated into a form of laxity. It was as though since he was not flighty, he had resolved to keep his foot sewn into the ground for as long as he wanted. When teaching this exercise, one of the barriers I had to break was teaching him to move. I knew it you it would affect everything else I had to teach him, like the domino effect. I had to play the first card right. I taught him to move with a click.

Now, this helped with the yielding exercise. If I applied pressure to the girth and he didn't move, then I would simply inculcate a click, then he would move based on his wired response to that stimuli. This is a good way to get your horse to move if they are not attuned to it. Continue the sequence until they move, and eventually, they would move without the direct sensation of your hand on the girth.

The key: Steady the horse and get them to move with a little stability around the forequarters.

## TURNING HINDQUARTERS

. . .

Here, we want to get the shoulders moving around the hindquarters. I like to use a dressage whip for this activity. Stand in a position where you can reach the shoulder of the horse with a dressage whip. Tap a little to get the attention of the horse. The aim is to get a step. If they don't move, apply more pressure to the horse or bump them. I have had to deal with some horses that required more than a bump, which is essentially a push. Let them move. Some trainers like to allow the horse to make a full circle, before rewarding them. However, your pressure and release duration and methodology should be tailored to the temperament of your horse. These exercises are useful for when you want to ride, as hand pressures are more easily responded to than saddles and stirrups- it gives ground for the establishment of a foundational trust.

It goes without saying, anything you do on the left should also be done on the right. This ensures balance and equality on each side of your horse.

# Backing Up

Yes, we love our horses. They are beautiful, they may serve one purpose or another, ranging from sportsmanship to personal use. They give a sense of grandeur and sometimes, we feel as though they are a core, important part of our lives. Horses have greatly improved my mental health. In the blinding heat of anxiety, I have ridden a horse to purge myself of fear. I have taken long slow walks on a horse, ruminating on important decisions in my head. I had my horse nuzzle up against my shoulder when they sensed I was in a depressive state. Horses have given, and they continue to give. However, as with most things, there is always a tendency to go overboard.

*Backing up a horse is one of the fundamental exercises used to establish gentle leadership.*

The purpose of the backing-up exercise is to teach the horse to develop respect for your personal space. Horses may be frightful and possible to tame, but we must never forget that they are quite large animals, and leaving a foot under a hoof has never been a good experience. Horses are sometimes biters, kickers, or downright malicious. With backing up, we want them to understand that there should be a security distance between them and us unless, of course, we demand otherwise. Just like with other exercises, your horse will learn to back up when you ask if you judiciously practice this exercise. There is nothing as fulfilling as finally cracking your horse, and being able to control it with one simple instruction, as opposed to wearing yourself out and running in circles with your horse.

The more you practice, the more responsive your horse will be. Additionally, you would not need to hold the rope to enforce a safe distance, and you will be able to instruct them to back up from the side, or from behind.

First of all, place yourself in front of the horse only if you have established a level of trust and you know the horse well. We do not want a situation where the horse charges at us or tries to run away and automatically barges into you. Remember your safety also comes first.

With a green horse, or what some might typically call a "problem horse," you should place yourself on a parallel line, but still in front of the horse. In the case of a dominating horse, you may want to keep your flag to push the horse away if it is necessary.

***Beginning the process:***

.    .    .

Gently raise your hands at the level of the horse's eyes. This move is primarily to catch the attention of the horse and let them know that we are about to begin work. Next, begin to wiggle your hand in a soft, steady manner. This should be adequate for the horse to feel the weight of the rope balancing snugly on his chin. Remember that we are prioritizing patience and trust. To this effect, you also have to shake the rope a little bit in order for the horse to understand and digest the cue.

It is normal for some horses to remain unmoved, and they fail to respond. In this case, be gentle or firm. If they move, release the pressure, and pet them. It is important to leave a few seconds before returning to perform other aspects of this exercise. This is to allow the horse to internalize what you have just taught them. Then, start over again in a structured pattern.

Soon, your horse will understand that he has to back up on the first cue, to avoid an uncomfortable bumping. It all boils down to making the wrong thing difficult for your horse to do, and the right thing easy. It may take just a few minutes for some horses to understand the exercise and respond accordingly, others it may take much longer. Backing up is a good illustration of one of the principles of horsemanship we discussed in book one of this series.

In their world, there is the need to establish yourself as number one. Number two is always the one who caves in to pressure and moves their feet first. You do not want to do that. Just like children, horses will want to continually test your boundaries. They will want to see how far they can go, how much you can be irked, and the level of disrespect you can let slide. It is our responsibility to guide them right in a gentle but firm way. In horses, the one who backs up follows the other. Therefore, make sure you are never the first to back up at any point in time!

Usually, with a level-headed and balanced horse, when you try this exercise on the second day, you will get a favorable response. Backing up seeps into every aspect of our lives with horses, apart from the need to create our personal space. Sometimes you may want to back the horse out of a trailer. Other times, it comes in handy to steady your horse if it is the type that moves forward when you throw on a saddle.

### *"What if My Horse Does Not Move?"*

When we discussed the leg yield, my response to trouble-shoot this problem, was to inculcate your cue for the horse to move into the exercise. However, it may be different with backing up. The click should not be used carelessly so as not to confuse the horses. Also, we do not want them moving forward or sideways as it would be counterproductive to the aim we are trying to achieve. When trying to get them to back up, many horses will be reluctant at the beginning because they are intelligent enough to know that the moment they step back, you are bestowed with dominance over them. For this reason, you have to be consistent and alert enough to reward any gentle yielding behavior.

. . .

'Dominance', of course, may seem like such a strong word. But, remember that the main goal is fair leadership, not tyranny. You do not want your horse to fear you. You want it to trust you. Every time he gives you the expected result, release pressure, pet, and let the horse be for some seconds. The timing for rest should not be too long as they have the propensity to forget the lesson you have just taught them. If it was hard for your horse to give up, a minute or two should be allotted to enable them to calm down.

Horses that did not work for a while or remained in the pasture for a few days or weeks, might be reluctant at the beginning of the session. You will have to be firm. Make sure you NEVER act with anger. It is easy to get frustrated when it seems like your efforts are not yielding any rewards. Anger is the worst feeling as a horse trainer, and you must resist it at all points. Anger blinds your judgment and makes you prone to mistakes. It makes you act without thinking, and what typically arises from it is regret. Your horse should show respect to your status, but not cower to your anger. In this context, you and your horse make a herd. Remind him that you are the leader of the head.

Some horses try to avoid pressure by moving right or left. The most dominating horses might even try to move forward and run over you. In that case, you will employ the use of a flag. Keep the flag in hand and push the horse away by waving it under his chin, or tapping his breast. If this does not work, that means you have to lunge the horse first. For the horses who try to move to the right or left, you have to remember that the head of the horse is in alignment with his body and your own position. Timing is important as you have to pull the head right back in place at the very second the horse tries to move around you. Before long, the horse will learn that backing up is the way to be at peace.

I have seen situations where I tell clients to perform exercises by standing in front of their horse, and the first thing they do is *walk around* their horse and put themselves in a particular position. This position they assume is where they would end up in the course of the exercise. They do this instead of asking the horse to move to a position where it can standstill. The crux of backing up at a distance has many applications. One day, I was at the barn grooming my horse. While doing so, I bent over to pick up a set of brushes. My horse most probably sensed this as abnormal behavior, and what she did was try to get closer to me. She probably sensed falsely that something was wrong. Another scenario could have been that she would begin to wander off because my attention was not on her. I made her back up, and still returned to pick up my brushes.

In backing up from a distance, we want to start from the widest point that we can. Just as previously mentioned, you have to engage your rope in this exercise. Raise your hands at a level that is at the bottom of the horse's nose. Don't be over the top with raising the rope. If the horse does not respond after several tries, you may have to move your feet forward. If the horse moves to the side, bump him in the right direction. Another method to try is swinging the lead rope as you try to back up the horse. Keep in mind that if you are going to make contact while using the lead rope, you should keep an average distance between you and the horse.

. . .

As we have previously reiterated, teaching your horse to back up is one of the most important lessons we can undertake. It is life-saving, and it grants you ease when performing basic tasks like grooming or loading into a trailer.

## Flexing

When we begin riding our horses, we are bound to come across circles and corners. We teach our horses flexion in order to prepare them before asking for a bend. Flexion is one of the elements in building a solid foundation for your horse.

Once you have mastered the act of flexion, your horse will no longer need your inside rein as a steering aid. In the absence of flexion, you will find that there is no direction, flexibility, or control radiating from your horse's body. Flexion can be longitudinal, vertical, or lateral.

Lateral flexion is sometimes called one rein stop. It is usually the first step in teaching your horses control with direction. This exercise can eventually translate into turning and rollbacks for your horse. When it comes to maintaining balance, you cannot ignore the place of lateral flexion. Lateral flexion as the name implies will be done either to the left or to the right.

I have worked with some horses who I may never want to spend another second with. There have been clashes of ego, the need to overcome my own fear and prejudices, and the never- ending test of my patience. Sometimes, I think the reason why cowboys are romanticized so heavily is not just for their looks, but also for the innate softness and tenderness that lies beneath the tanned and rough palms. When you work with animals, you learn to speak another language and break through the barrier of mere words. Horses changed me and made me a better person. Maybe cowboy romance stories are not so corny after all! Where am I going with this story? I had a hard time giving my horse a thorough understanding of lateral flexion. However, once I got the right way to do it, the lesson stuck.

First, I will start by explaining the 'tail hair' method. The tail hair can be replaced by a piece of string. I should warn that if you have a horse that drags you all over the place and who you have not established a footing with, it may be difficult to do this exercise. In the old days, there was a test to prove how good a horseman you are, and how light your horse is. So, they would tie the bridle reins under the beard, with nothing but five pieces of horse hair. If one were to break the five pieces of horse hair, then it would be said that you were pulling too hard on the rein, or your horse wasn't light.

In the tail hair method, you tie the lead rope to the halter with one single strand of tail hair or string. Stand sideways at the level of the shoulder, then gently pick up the rope just right by the horse's nose. Then, wait for the horse to move towards it with its nose, and let go when they do. This exercise heavily prioritizes gentleness and patience. In most cases, you have to wait for a longer time than expected for the horse to turn. Repeat this exercise. Keep in mind that on your first try, your horse may not turn all the way around. You have to be attentive to know when they are making the slightest move towards turning, and then, let go of the rope. The left ear may move towards you before the head turns around, and that is a good sign that your horse is making an attempt.

The sequence goes this way;

*Pick up the rope. Wait. Let go of it.*

It is that simple.

"How Hard Do I Have to Pull?"

Many clients come with this question. The straightforward answer is, to hold the rope in such a way that you would be unaware of any pull. The string is a guide to let you know that the exercise should be handled carefully, but firmly. The firmness should lean towards assertiveness in your body language and proper control of the situation. At this point, we already know that horses sense such energies.

## TEACHING LATERAL FLEXION TO A WARMBLOOD

With warmbloods, there might be modifications to the approach we would typically take on other horses, for safety reasons, and also to ensure that they learn properly. During the exercise, you want to make sure that your horse doesn't pull on the lead rope if you are leading him or doing the groundwork.

The major difference when dealing with warmbloods is the horseman's eagerness to release the gentle pull and wait. Warmbloods also have a tendency to have much more forward impulsion than a stock horse would. If the horse begins to move its feet, hold on to the rope until they stop and move their heads, and then you can let go.

Warmbloods are pulsing with energy and often want to run around. If your horse has difficulty standing still, do not attempt this exercise until it is in a position to listen to you. You may test your horse's willingness to do this by touching and rubbing it down with the rope to gauge its response.

Continue the exercise and note that when the horse's ears become more even towards you, it is a good sign. I have noticed situations where the horse begins to drop its head or turn in the opposite direction. The solution to this is to simply hold on until they turn towards you, then reward that correct behavior.

A lot of horses are stiff all the way through to their spine. They travel without any type of bend or flexibility. Sometimes, while supposedly traveling straight, their posture is still crooked because they are overbuilt on one side. Flexing is a good way to get them more symmetric in their muscles. It provides benefits for not just the horse, but also you, its owner.

# Lunging For Respect

Every instruction in this book is explained sequentially. This is evidenced in the fact that before you lunge your horse, you have to make sure that it can flex to the left and to the right. You want to make sure that they can flex slightly in both directions. The horse should also know how to respond to the forward cue.

There is an interesting background story to why it is called a 'lunge'. The word is believed to be derived from French or Latin. The French word, 'allonge', means to lengthen. The Latin word, 'longa', means long- this is in its most basic form, Pilates for horses! Lunging is useful for calming high-strung horses and gaining control. We can see how the etymology of the word is applied in real life. Horse lunging is a training method that involves having the horse move in a large circumference.

. . .

If you are hearing about it for the first time, you may be tempted to picture a horse on a yoga mat, leaning forward with one knee bent. Thankfully, this is not the case. When lunging, a horse works at the end of a long lead rope which is the lunge line, and it moves in a circular motion as the owner gives out instructions. The length of the lunge line can range from 7.6 meters to 10 meters long.

You may want to draw a circle on the ground of the round pen for the horse to follow while doing this exercise. This is not a prerequisite, but it does help some clients. You would need the lead rope and a lunge whip. Have the horse do a forward cue, flex, and tap the hindquarters. The horse may begin to go around you while still maintaining that flexion. Keep the horse doing this for a short while and if it stops, tap on the hindquarters again and watch the horse pick up moving.

"What If My Horse Knocks Me Over With Its Shoulder?"

There are some things that could go wrong while practicing lunging. However, every problem is paired with a solution. In this case, when you hold the rope, make sure the nose is turned towards you. And if the horse does turn into you, is to push to its side a little bit. The horse will essentially perform a side pass while bowing to your pressure.

Once your horse gets the lunging memo, reward and remember to repeat the action on the other side. Make sure that the horse is going around you, and you are not the one going around your horse. Make the circles bigger as you repeat this exercise. Over time, the horse would break into a canter around the circle as they get better. To change direction, push your hands with the whip, have the horse stop, before resuming in the other direction.

## BENEFITS OF LUNGING

I had a horse who was what you could conveniently call a cold back. Trying to mount it always seemed like an impossibly hard task, because he always bucked. I had just taken one of the regular classes I took, and when I got back, I taught him what I learned about lunging. I would put the saddle on and work him on the lunge before riding. Soon, the bucking issue disappeared. There are a lot of benefits to lunging your horse.

1. *It can help calm hyperactive horses*

There is nothing suitable for blowing off steam like a good old lunge. Also, when you have not ridden your horse for a while, they are prone to anxiety or being a bit "fresh," (easily excitable). The exercise can serve as a warm-up to get them in a good state of mind before riding. Warmbloods are full of adrenaline, and working a lunge can help tone down their fervor and keep you safe while riding.

1. *It strengthens communication*

Lunging can help to get your horse accustomed to your voice and body language. Since the handler is in a situation where a lot of instructions are issued, more cues are used and the horse is given a chance to see how you operate. This is why it is advised to maintain a confident posture, and the body language of a leader when doing any exercise.

1. *It helps ill or recovering horses*

This type of horse cannot be ridden. Lunging the horse is a good alternative to keep them alert and remind them that you are there along with maintaining body conditioning.

1. *It paves a smoother path for learning horse riding*

1. *It helps horses get used to equipment used in riding*

1. *It is essential for training and conditioning*

Lunging cuts across all forms of training. Your horse can be trained to leap, reverse, stretch, etc. it is also used to introduce the younger horses to voice cues. It is a good base for more complicated training.

. . .

"When is Lunging Considered Bad?"

Lunging can be counterproductive when it is not done the right way. There is nothing inherently bad about it, but some errors can occur, such as lunging for an extended period of time. A good baseline is 30 minutes, and this varies between horses. In some cases, 4-6 minutes could be enough. Doing it too much can cause joint strain in your horse.

Another mistake that could be made is lunging without a whip. There would be no outlet for your disapproval to be communicated. Furthermore, lunging in a small circle can be restrictive. Lastly, another mistake made is lunging without giving thought to how you can protect yourself. Wear gloves, avoid the kick zone, and watch the rope so that it does not get entangled in the hooves.

In conclusion, this book has been able to establish the critical horse training methods, from desensitization to lunging. I am confident that it will help in your journey with your horse. Godspeed! If this book has benefitted you, I would greatly appreciate a review. If you think this book may be beneficial to someone you know, please feel free to share this book with them and encourage them to gain a better understanding of some horsemanship and training fundamentals.

Made in the USA
Middletown, DE
01 September 2022

72914506R00090